encyclopedia of
canaries
by g.t. dodwell

All photos by Harry V. Lacey unless indicated otherwise.

Cover; Front:
Border Fancy canary. Photo by Harry V. Lacey.

Cover, back:
Scotch Fancy canary. Photo by Harry V. Lacey.

Frontispiece:
Frilled cock. Photo by Harry V. Lacey.

ISBN 0-87666-952-6

Distributed in the U.S.A. by T.F.H. Publications, Inc., 211 West Sylvania Avenue, P.O. Box 27, Neptune City, N.J. 07753; in England by T.F.H. (Gt. Britain) Ltd., 13 Nutley Lane, Reigate, Surrey; in Canada to the book store and library trade by Clarke, Irwin & Company, Clarwin House, 791 St. Clair Avenue West, Toronto 10, Ontario; in Canada to the pet trade by Rolf C. Hagen Ltd., 3225 Sartelon Street, Montreal 382, Quebec; in Southeast Asia by Y.W. Ong, 9 Lorong 36 Geylang, Singapore 14; in Australia and the south Pacific by Pet Imports Pty. Ltd., P.O. Box 149, Brookvale 2100, N.S.W., Australia. Published by T.F.H. Publications Inc. Ltd., The British Crown Colony of Hong Kong.

CONTENTS

INTRODUCTORY

THE CANARY FANCY.....................................5
HISTORY...8
    Origin. . . Early Variations. . . Origin of Local Breeds. . .
    Early Fanciers. . . The Nineteenth Century. . . Recent History

GENERAL MANAGEMENT

HOUSING AND EQUIPMENT..........................17
    Aviaries. . . Birdrooms. . . Cages. . . Cage Fittings. . . Other
    Appliances
FEEDING AND GENERAL MANAGEMENT...............32
    Types of Food. . . Food for Canaries. . . Management
BREEDING — PRACTICAL............................47
    Breeding Systems. . . Breeding Season Accessories. . . Pairing
    . . . Nest Building. . . Egg Laying. . . Incubation. . . Weaning
    . . . Ringing. . . Second Broods. . . Care of Young Stock
BREEDING — THEORY...............................73
    Heredity and Environment. . . The Mechanism of Heredity
    . . . Mendelian Inheritance in Canaries. . . Variation. . .
    Selection. . . Breeding Methods. . . Practical Issues. . . Addi-
    tional Reading
MOLTING..90
    Time for Molting. . . The Molting Process. . . Caging. . .
    General Management. . . Feeding. . . Color Feeding. . . Con-
    clusion of the Molt
EXHIBITING......................................103
    Types of Exhibition. . . Show Cages and Cases. . . Training
    . . . Entering. . . Preparation. . . Dispatch. . . At the Show
DISEASES AND PARASITES.........................129
    Preventive Measures. . . Dealing with Sick Birds. . . Parasites
    . . . Disinfection. . . Additional Reading

VARIETIES

COLOR AND MARKINGS...........................141
    Basic Pigments. . . Variegation. . . Technical Markings. . .
    Buff. . . White Varieties. . . Age Differences. . . Sexing

THE BORDER FANCY 150
　　History. . . Description. . . Breeding. . . Molting. . . Exhibiting. . . Official Standard
THE YORKSHIRE 160
　　History. . . Description. . . Breeding. . . Molting. . . Exhibiting. . . Official Standard
THE NORWICH 179
　　History. . . Description. . . Breeding. . . Molting. . . Exhibiting. . . Official Standard
THE GLOSTER FANCY 195
　　History. . . Description. . . Breeding. . . Molting. . . Exhibiting. . . Official Standard
THE LIZARD 203
　　History. . . Description. . . Breeding. . . Molting. . . Exhibiting. . . Official Standard
OTHER VARIETIES OF BRITISH ORIGIN 213
　　The Crested Canary. . . The Fife Fancy. . . The Lancashire . . . The London Fancy. . . The Scotch Fancy
VARIETIES FROM CONTINENTAL EUROPE 227
　　The Belgian. . . Frilled Canaries
CANARIES IN NORTH AMERICA (by Dr. Val Clear).......247
　　Judging Rollers. . . Judging the Domestic Hartz. . . The Columbus Fancy. . . Developing the American Singer Canary . . . Judging American Singers. . . The National Association
THE RED FACTOR AND OTHER NEW COLORS 261
　　The Dilute. . . The Recessive White. . . The Dominant White . . . The Red Factor. . . The Dimorphic. . . The Citron. . . Recent Mutations
THE ROLLER 272
　　History. . . Description. . . Breeding. . . Training. . . Exhibiting. . . Official Standard
INDEX 283

INTRODUCTORY

1

The Canary Fancy

The newcomer to the canary fancy is the inheritor of the great traditions in livestock breeding which, in one form or another, man has developed in various parts of the world. In the case of animals of economic importance this tradition is perhaps taken for granted but it is equally true of the canary. The Norwich, Belgian, Border Fancy or Dutch Frill breeds are just as well known to canary enthusiasts all over the world as are the Hereford and Jersey among cattle breeders, the Merino and Southdown to sheep specialists, or the Leghorn and Rhode Island Red to poultry men.

Past generations of breeders, through whose skill and patience the various types of canary were conceived and developed, have left a wonderful legacy of living material in the hands of the hobbyists of today and it should be the earnest desire of all who enter the fancy to live up to the high standards of former times.

One of the outstanding attractions of the hobby of canary keeping is that it has an interest all through the year. There is always something going on and well marked seasons lead from one to another so that no single aspect ever has a chance of becoming tedious. Activities may be said to begin with the breeding season which extends from the end of March until about the end of June or the middle of July in England. Because of hot summer weather in the United States many breeders mate their canaries on February 14, Valentine's Day. It is desirable to finish the breeding season by the end of June at the very latest. This is followed by the molting season which carries on until about mid-October. Soon after this the main show season is beginning to get under way and continues until January after which the fancier has a much needed breathing spell for the overhaul and spring cleaning of his cages and equipment, the conditioning of his stock birds, and for the general routine preparation for the new breeding season.

A special point of recommendation for the beginner is that in this hobby he has a real chance of achieving success without the outlay of unreasonable sums of money. Financial considerations of course are not generally uppermost in the mind of anyone who is attracted to a particular hobby but naturally in the majority of cases they cannot be disregarded altogether. The canary fancy is ideal in this respect since it suits all pockets and the fancier can spend just as much or as little as he feels he can afford.

Canaries can be bred just as successfully in an attic or spare room as in the most lavishly furnished birdroom and they are among the cheapest of all livestock to feed. A single canary consumes something in the region of 1½ to 2 ounces of seed a week, plus small additions in the way of greenstuff and softfood, so that a couple of dozen birds can be maintained for far less than it would cost to keep a dog or a cat.

Much of the equipment needed for the hobby is not difficult to construct and, although obtainable ready made from fanciers' suppliers if desired, is well within the capabilities of the average handyman. Neither need the purchase of the initial stock impose any great financial strain. High figures have no doubt been paid from time to time for outstanding birds, as is the case in most branches of livestock keeping, but good sound average specimens of most breeds are usually quite reasonably priced and well within the reach of the fancier of moderate or limited means.

Although canary keeping is essentially a hobby that is carried on at home it is not without its social aspects too. A fancier can of course, should he so wish, carry out his pursuit in complete isolation and with a minimum of contact with his fellow hobbyists but thereby many useful associations are lost. It should be the aim of every newcomer to become a member of his local cage bird society and to share his experiences with others as they will with him.

These local clubs are the backbone of the hobby and are to be found in many towns of reasonable size in all parts of the country. Their activities are many. Regular meetings of the members are held throughout the year at which lectures, film shows, exchange of stock, judging competitions and similar useful and instructive activities take place. Visits to neighboring clubs are made, outings arranged to birdkeeping establishments of particular interest and in most cases an annual show is staged during the course of the year for the participation of members.

Later on the fancier will probably wish to join one of the specialist societies which cater for his own favorite breed. There are a number of these and they fulfill an important role in the fancy by fostering the interests of the specialist breeder and encouraging the improvement and exhibiting of their particular fancy variety.

Of recent years the phenomenal rise in the popularity of the budgerigar has perhaps threatened the once secure position of the canary considered purely as a household pet, but in the realms of fancying it still reigns supreme. Canary breeders continue to be the mainstay of the majority of cage bird societies and at shows held during the autumn and winter months the canary section usually outnumbers that of the other birds.

Although various works on specialized aspects of the hobby have appeared from time to time during the past decade, few books embracing the whole field of canary culture have been published. Most of the old standard works have long since been out of print and copies of them are therefore scarce and usually difficult to obtain. It is hoped that the present volume, while not attempting to rival in sheer mass of detail the great English Victorian and Edwardian classics on the subject, will at least cover most of the groundwork for the enthusiastic beginner and perhaps prove of some value even to those of greater experience.

2

History

The average canary fancier of today is perhaps not unduly concerned with the fascinating history that lies behind his hobby. Not unnaturally he tends to be much more preoccupied with this year's show program or next season's breeding prospects rather than with the origins of the domestic canary or with developments that took place too long ago to have any significance for him. This is rather a pity since a knowledge of the historical background of any hobby can add enormously to its enjoyment.

A comparison of the diversity of form to be found in the highly developed modern varieties with the somewhat insignificant wild canary must inevitably arouse feelings of respect for what has been achieved in the past, especially when it is realized that, as domestic creatures go, the canary is a comparatively recent introduction. Most of the animals of survival value to man have been associated with him often for thousands of years but canary keeping, implying as it does a fair standard of civilization with sufficient leisure to enjoy such pursuits, has a history of only about 450 years. It is, however, only during the past 150 years or so that we have any reasonably detailed records; before this there are large gaps in our knowledge with only a few of the important landmarks known.

ORIGIN

The wild canary which was the progenitor of all our domestic breeds was first introduced into Europe from the Canary Islands by the Spaniards, probably commencing soon after the final conquest of the islands in 1495, although it is possible that some may have been brought over before this date. They are still to be found wild in many of the western islands of the group, as well as in Madeira and the Azores, and an account of their distribution and habits is to be found in D.A. Bannerman's *Birds of the Atlantic Islands*. It has been said that at first only the male birds were allowed to be exported so as to prevent the species being bred in captivity and thus protecting the very profitable trade of the bird catchers but it is far more likely that it was only the males that were in any demand on account of their accomplishments as songsters.

The earliest known reference to the bird in the literature of natural history is in Gesner's *Historia Animalium* published in Zurich during the years 1551-1558 where, having dealt with the citril, he adds, "Similar to this, so I hear, is the bird of sweetest song called the canary which is brought from the Canary Islands". This, together with remarks by other authors, makes it clear that the canary was quite well known in Europe by the latter half of the sixteenth century.

In the past authorities have tended to differ on the precise scientific status of the wild canary but nowadays the most generally accepted view is that it is one of the races of the serin and it has been given the subspecific title of *Serinus canarius canarius*. Its nearest relatives are the serin (*S.c. serinus*) and the Syrian wild canary (*S.c. syriacus*).

Many people find it hard to believe that such a diversity of type such as is found in our domestic canaries could possibly have had one source alone and it has sometimes been argued that they must owe their origin to the interbreeding of more than one species. That such a suggestion is not impossible has been adequately proved in recent years by the introduction of the Red Factor canary which is known to be of hybrid origin, and it is certainly true that in the early days of canary keeping the knowledge of birds generally was often insufficiently accurate to recognize racial, and sometimes even specific, differences. In the absence of any definite evidence to the contrary however it must be accepted that the domestic bird has descended solely from the wild stock imported into Europe from the islands previously referred to.

9

EARLY VARIATIONS

At what stage fanciers actually began to breed canaries in captivity rather than to rely on imported birds is not known although it would appear to be early in the seventeenth century. In 1622 the writer Olina stated that, at that time, not only were they being successfully bred in Italy, but also that they even had an annual surplus of birds that were sent to Germany, Switzerland and the Tyrol. Other confirmation of their domestication came from the English writer Joseph (or Josiah) Blagrove in 1675 when, after saying that they bred canaries "very plentifully" in Germany and Italy, added that "they have also bred some few here in England though as yet not anything to the purpose that they do in other countries". Evidently the birds at that time had shown no tendency to depart from the wild form for Blagrove stated that most people could not distinguish a canary "from one of our common green birds."—i.e. greenfinches.

How or when variation first occurred cannot be determined but even among wild birds cinnamon, albino and melanistic mutations are occasionally found so that such variants could have been present at times among wild-caught imported birds in the early days, although it is doubtful whether they would have been perpetuated. The artificial conditions of housing and feeding which are necessarily imposed by breeding in captivity were a much more likely source of influence upon any departure from the normal as can be seen in the pied or broken color patterns in many species of domestic livestock. Even this does not usually occur until domestication has been in progress for many years and it was not until 1709 that any mention of variation in the canary was made.

In this year the first important work on the canary, the *Traite des Serins de Canarie*, was published in France and written by Hervieux who was the superintendent of the aviaries and poultry yards to the Duchesse de Berry. This book was the first standard authority on canaries and went through several editions during the eighteenth century, also being translated into other languages.

Hervieux listed 29 varieties but a critical study of them

reveals that they were not actually distinct breeds as we would understand them today but merely a number of plumage variations that had become sufficiently well established at that time. Many of them are easy to identify by his descriptions as the self, foul and variegated canaries, both green and cinnamon, that are recognized by fanciers today; but some of them are difficult to interpret unless they represented some unusual mutations which have since been lost to us.

One thing that can be safely inferred from the list however is the fact that by the beginning of the eighteenth century the canary had developed a number of variations in its plumage and that even completely clear yellow birds had already occurred which Hervieux said at that date were the most rare.

ORIGIN OF LOCAL BREEDS

Although we have no information on the subject, the evolution of breeds of different *type*, as distinct from the mere plumage variants, was probably already beginning. Many of our old breeds are known to have had their roots in the eighteenth century and two of them at least were already well established and clearly described in an old manual dated 1762.

Most breeds of livestock, even though they may since have acquired a world wide reputation, were essentially local in their origins, as is clearly indicated by the names under which they are still known, and the reason is not difficult to understand. It will be readily appreciated that in those days, before the improvement of roads or the coming of the railways, communications were so poor that the chances of fanciers meeting together other than on an extremely local basis was virtually impossible. This isolation would lead eventually to the production of recognizable types of bird that appealed generally to the tastes of the groups of breeders who found it possible to meet with reasonable ease.

Simple selection on a visual basis would probably have been the only breeding principle known to these old fanciers and this method allied, by necessity or design, to a certain amount of inbreeding would lead in due course to a fair degree of genetic stability being reached and a true-breeding distinctive local type would therefore become established. The further development of these original breeds following their spread to other parts is a later story.

EARLY FANCIERS

As with the bird itself regrettably little is known about the hobby of bird keeping in its early days. Most writers on birds were ornithologists rather than aviculturalists and we learn nothing from them apart from the facts already given that canaries were well known in Europe, first as imported birds and later on bred on some scale. It is almost certain however that, in common with other birds, they were most likely to have been kept originally by the more well-to-do type of person in aviaries as an added attraction to their gardens or country estates.

It would appear that the actual breeding of canaries in cages and the emergence of a distinct "fancy" as we would understand it took place largely during the eighteenth century and was mainly due to the activities of working people as distinct from the more leisured classes. Over a period of many years artisans from continental Europe, such as the Flemish weavers from the Low Countries and the Huguenot refugees from France, went to settle in England taking much of their culture with them and it was from this class of person that the idea of fancying as a hobby seems to have come and spread to others with whom they had contact—not only in connection with canaries, of course, but with other kinds of small livestock and horticulture as well.

This period of history apparently also saw the formation of the first canary clubs for, in an English article on the subject of the canary fancy in the *Illustrated London News* of December 12, 1846 it was stated that societies had then been in existence in the city for "upwards of a century". Societies devoted to the culture of the canary were also known in Belgium in the early 1800's.

THE NINETEENTH CENTURY

Although the origins of the hobby are based in the eighteenth century it was during the following 100 years that its greatest development took place. From the sparsely recorded beginnings of the early days to the well documented organization at the close of the century is a story of continual progress. The article in the *Illustrated London News*, already referred to, and a delightful book called *The Canary, Its Varieties, Management and Breeding* by the Rev. Francis Smith, both give an insight into the fancy as it was in the early part and the middle years of the century in London and Manchester respectively but the greatest period of progress was to come later.

The general improvement in Britain's prosperity during the second half of the nineteenth century became reflected in the hobby and some of the oldest cage bird societies that are still in existence and flourishing today were founded during these times. More commonly, however, cage birds were only one section of the general fanciers' societies which were usually devoted also to poultry, pigeons, rabbits and other small livestock, but the great attraction of small birds at the mixed shows that were held eventually led to demands for separate societies.

The last quarter of the century in particular saw a great expansion of the bird fancy which continued right up to the first World War and although by then most of the very old canary clubs of the eighteenth and early nineteenth centuries had become defunct many newer societies of a general nature as well as specialist societies catering for each particular breed had sprung up to take their place. The improving social conditions of those days, together with the spread of education and better means of communication, produced a more articulate individual who not only formed cage bird societies and kept proper records of their activities but also began to create a demand for text books and periodicals about his hobby. This period therefore became notable for the publication in England of the first really comprehensive works of reference on cage birds. Foremost among these were *The Canary Book* by R.L. Wallace and the superb *Book of Canaries and Cage Birds*, published by Cassell's, in which the section on canaries was written by W.A. Blakston, the leading authority of this era. From such works as these can still be gleaned a wealth of practical advice from the times of our grandfathers and great-grandfathers much of which has not been superseded even to this day.

The period from about 1880 onwards also saw great changes in many of the breeds themselves. The increasing popularity of canaries, the formation of new societies and the publication of books and fanciers' journals all led to a freer exchange of ideas and greater flexibility of thought than had been possible in earlier years and progressive breeders began to appreciate qualities in other varieties that could lead to an improvement in their own. Having put their ideas into practice a trend was set in motion which the rank and file were not slow to follow and eventually no breed, except perhaps the Lizard, became free from the effects of crossbreeding so that by and large modern varieties are often somewhat different from their forebears of a century ago.

RECENT HISTORY

Except for the obvious setbacks occasioned by two major world wars, the momentum gained by the canary fancy during the latter part of the previous century has continued to the present day and it is probably true to say that, in spite of the numerous counter attractions of the modern world, the hobby is as flourishing now as it ever was.

The demands of fanciers for regular literature on the subject has led to the publication of weekly and monthly periodicals devoted entirely to cage birds and further important books appearing about canaries since the Victorian classics include *Canaries, Hybrids and British Birds* edited by S.H. Lewer (1911), *Our Canaries* by Claude St. John (1911) and *Canaries* by C.A. House (1923). In addition to these larger works, many smaller handbooks have appeared from time to time, often monographs on one particular breed or dealing with other specialized aspects of the canary fancy.

As in the previous era the twentieth century has also witnessed important changes in the canary itself—not always agreeable ones. In particular the final extinction of certain of the old-fashioned breeds has taken place and some others are lingering on in such small numbers as to make their continued existence precarious to say the least. On the credit side

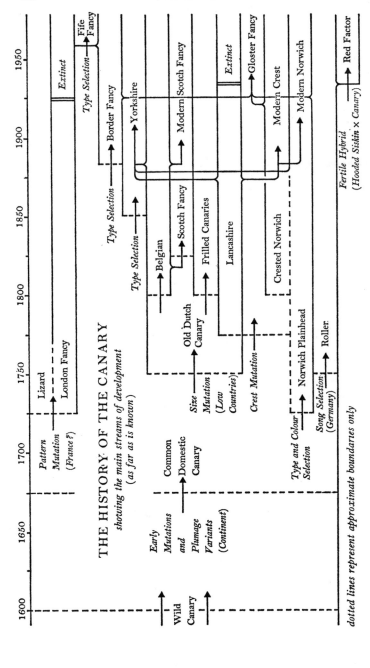

THE HISTORY OF THE CANARY

showing the main streams of development
(as far as is known)

dotted lines represent approximate boundaries only

15

however we have seen the creation of some new varieties of great merit which have already achieved considerable popularity while what might be termed the "standard breeds" continue to receive solid support which is bound to keep them in the forefront for many years to come.

The chief attributes of the canary which have received the attention of fanciers during its long period as a domestic bird can be summarized under the headings of *type* (i.e. its shape or form), *color*, and *song* and, in the chapters that follow, the various breeds are dealt with in that sequence. Owing to the fact that the bird was first domesticated in Europe most breeds of the canary are of European origin where English fanciers, in particular, have excelled in the realms of type and most of the classic breeds of today are of their raising. Recognition must also be given to the significant contributions made by Dutch, Belgian, French and Italian fanciers in the area of Frilled canaries, to the Spanish for producing the Timbrado, the Germans for creating the Hartz or Roller, and to the North Americans for the American Singer or Warbler. The persons who worked for years in the development of the various breeds are largely unknown and unsung but the entire canary fancy is indebted to them. It is only by continuing with the work done by such dedicated and creative people that progress in the canary fancy can be made.

GENERAL MANAGEMENT

3

Housing and Equipment

For those who have decided to take up the breeding of canaries as a hobby, although there is a very natural desire to possess some birds at the earliest possible moment, the first question that ought to be considered is that of providing a suitable place in which to carry on one's activities. Few, perhaps, will have sufficient funds to allow them the luxury of an unlimited choice in this matter, but every newcomer will naturally wish to do the very best he can for his charges by providing them with such accommodation within his means as will ensure their maximum well-being. It is true to say that canaries are extremely adaptable creatures and have been known to succeed under quite unsuitable conditions, but to expect them to do so consistently is not only unreasonable but is bound to end ultimately in disappointment. It will be found that much of the pleasure to be derived from canary keeping comes from the satisfaction of doing the job well, and it cannot be denied that success is far more likely to follow if the birds are kept in as nearly perfect conditions as circumstances will allow.

AVIARIES

To the general public the place for keeping birds is an aviary which, by definition, is a structure allowing the birds complete freedom of flight within the limits of the space provided, be it large or small. In certain circumstances such a method of bird keeping may be quite adequate, particularly where the object is merely to add to the general attractions of a garden by accommodating such birds as will give pleasure by their varied colors and song. It is also possible to produce a fair number of birds of a reasonable standard by the method known as colony breeding, in which a few cock birds are allowed to run with a larger number of hens during the breeding season. If the initial stock is of high quality there is no reason why satisfactory results should not be obtained in this way, but genuine pedigree breeding is clearly not possible under such conditions.

The general housing of exhibition canaries in aviaries however, is not to be recommended for a variety of reasons. Foremost of these is the lack of control that can be exercised during the breeding season, where, even if one has taken the trouble of pairing the birds preparatory to their release into the aviary, it cannot be guaranteed that they will remain with the same partners as planned, so that the keeping of accurate records becomes an impossibility. Added to this, the birds tend to get somewhat out of hand during the period spent in an aviary, and when brought into cages once more the problem of steadying them down again will arise. Further difficulties will be encountered if faults in carriage and posture are developed, as they are very prone to do under these conditions, for once they have become a habit they may prove troublesome to eradicate.

To the exhibition canary breeder, aviaries may occasionally be useful as a temporary home for young birds for the few weeks following their weaning, or possibly for the overwintering of his breeding stock, but only a minority of fanciers ever make use of them in this way.

BIRDROOMS
The only really satisfactory way of housing exhibition stock is to do so in cages within the confines of a room specially set aside for this purpose, and in this way complete control over the birds can be exercised at all times. Such rooms, specially fitted out for the hobby and known to fanciers as 'birdrooms', are practically universal in the canary world and may be of the indoor or outdoor variety. Whichever of the two types may finally be decided upon, the guiding principles to observe are that they should be free from

Above: Simple birdroom constructed from a garden shed. Below: Interior of same room above.

More elaborate birdroom with outdoor flights in an attractive garden setting.

damp, draughts, bad ventilation and fluctuating temperatures, plus being vermin proof, all these conditions being contrary to the well-being of canaries.

The Indoor Birdroom: This is generally a spare room in the house that has been adapted to the requirements of bird keeping and is most frequently the spare bedroom or, in older type properties, possibly the storeroom or attic. Convenience for one's hobby is often an important consideration, and to have the birds actually on the premises can be a distinct advantage especially during adverse weather conditions when a trip down the garden to an outdoor birdroom may not be particularly inviting. Many thousands of canaries are annually bred in such quarters and they have much to recommend them.

If there is any freedom of choice in the matter, following the principles mentioned above, the indoor birdroom should be the one that is well ventilated yet free from drafts, adequately lit and of a fairly equable temperature. The absence of dampness and of vermin would naturally be assumed in an indoor room. Ideally it should have an east or south-east aspect so that the birds would have the benefit of the morning sunshine and be spared the high temperature of late afternoon that might be experienced during a hot summer in a room facing south or south-west. At the same time, a room with the windows facing a busy road should be avoided, as the constantly flashing headlights of passing cars at night can be most disturbing to the birds and may well be responsible for unsuccessful breeding results.

Often very little needs to be done in the way of adapting an indoor room to the needs of canary keeping, the most obvious being the provision of some shelves or staging to hold the breeding cages. Usually at least two of the walls of the room can be used to accommodate these, which will still leave sufficient room for storing other equipment, and for a table which will be found useful for many of the tasks that need to be done when attending the birds. Safeguards against the accidental loss of any bird that might escape from its cage should include covering the window with ½-inch mesh wire netting. If this is attached to a light wooden framework, it is a simple matter to remove while the windows are being cleaned or adjusted for ventilation. If there is a fireplace in the room, it should be boarded up.

To prevent dust or seed husks from getting between the floor boards they can be covered with one of the modern floor covering materials which are very easy to keep clean and will add to the neat appearance of the room. Some provision should also be made to prevent husks and feathers from blowing under the door and so becoming a nuisance in other parts of the house.

The Outdoor Birdroom: In spite of the various advantages to be gained from an indoor birdroom it is usually the ultimate ambition of every fancier to possess an outdoor birdroom for his hobby and in many cases this is the only possible way for him to keep birds, especially in the smaller modern house where no spare room is available. Provided that the structure is soundly made with careful attention to detail, this method of housing canaries is probably the most satisfactory and is widely used by experienced fanciers.

The outdoor birdroom can take many forms but in the majority of cases it is usually basically a garden shed type of building, but if something more decorative is needed it can be of an attractive summerhouse or garden chalet design. Some excellent birdrooms can also be made from the modern home-extension units, where, with careful planning, the advantages of both indoor and outdoor birdrooms can be combined. Many firms specializing in sectional buildings of all descriptions have a number of designs among their products that are admirably suited for fitting out as birdrooms, should the fancier wish to avail himself of a ready made structure. These firms flourish in England but do not exist in the United States.

A great many handymen however, will be more likely to enjoy building their own birdroom, but a raw beginner in the fancy would first be well advised to study as many structures of this nature as possible with a view to finding out from their owners any useful information, including possible pitfalls, that may help him in his own efforts. But whether it is decided to purchase a ready made building or to construct one's own, there are certain basic points that will need to be considered.

Size: The birdroom should be of adequate size for the number of birds it is eventually intended to keep. In all branches of livestock keeping, overcrowding is a potential danger to the health of the stock and in this canaries are no exception, but if cost is a limiting factor the design should be one that can easily be extended as and when circumstances warrant it. As a guide to what is required it may be assumed that a shed of 8 feet by 6 feet would accommodate approximately 48 birds if caged singly, or 60 birds if the hens were placed three together in double compartment cages. This is equivalent to six breeding pairs plus their maximum expected progeny of one year's breeding. Similarly a shed of 12 feet by

Successful conversion of an attic room for the hobby of canary breeding.

8 feet would accommodate 64 birds in single compartments, or 80 birds by the doubling up of the hens, an equivalent of eight breeding pairs and their expected progeny. To achieve such accommodation it would be necessary to utilize three inside walls for the cages and consequently the door would have to be in the front.

Design: It is always advisable to avoid elaborate designs in order to allow for greater ease in the management of the stock and for the maintenance of the fabric. It should be solid and well-built, as flimsy structures are much more liable to accidental damage and in course of time may even become distorted due to the warping of the materials. The building must also be vermin-proof so that no mice can gain admittance, otherwise they will disturb the birds and, more particularly, contaminate the seed if this is accessible.

On the question of flooring opinions are somewhat divided, some favoring concrete and others wood. The latter is really the better as concrete is liable to be cold and damp in winter. Ideally the birdroom should be raised well clear of the ground level, supported upon brick or concrete piers, thus allowing free circulation of air below with consequent freedom from any possibility of dampness.

Materials: The birdroom may be constructed of any materials suitable for outdoor buildings. A brick structure would obviously be very desirable but is likely to be far too expensive for all but the well-to-do, so that the most usual plan is to have a timber framed building clad in wood, asbestos sheeting or corrugated iron. The first is probably the most satisfactory, but in all cases an inside lining and good insulation would be necessary to avoid violently fluctuating temperatures. Efficient insulation of the roof is particularly important as it is here that heat is lost in the winter or penetrates when the sun is hot during the summer.

Ventilation: It is most important that there should be free circulation of fresh air without drafts and this can be readily provided if the air intakes are below, but not opposite, the level of the lowest cages, and the outlets are above the highest ones. All ventilators can be fitted with sliding covers if it should ever be thought necessary to restrict the flow of air at any time, although only in the very worst of weather is this likely to arise. An added refinement to the ventilation system is the provision of an extractor fan which can prove valuable in hot, sultry weather when even in the best ventilated rooms the air is apt to be at a standstill.

Lighting: What has already been said in respect to indoor rooms concerning this aspect is equally applicable to the outdoor birdroom, and if possible an east or south-east facing position is the ideal. Good lighting is essential for success so that plenty of window space should be allowed for. The majority of fanciers have to attend to their birds in the evenings after work, and this in the winter makes artificial lighting a necessity. Most of them agree that they would not use it if an alternative could be found, as artificial light at this time of year is unnatural and is liable to throw the birds out of condition. If installed at all, a dimming device is necessary in order to allow the birds to return naturally to their perches to roost after their wants have been attended to.

Heating: The question of heating the birdroom is one that will eventually arise, and on this matter fanciers are again divided in their opinions. Let it be said at once that although canaries originated in a warmer country they are now perfectly acclimatized and in normal circumstances should have no need for artificial heating. There is however, the fancier himself to be considered, and once he has experienced a spell of wintry weather when day after day the birds' water pots are frozen solid, he may well change his mind concerning the provision of some form of heat, not so much for the birds' benefit but his own. Many fanciers will also agree that it is desirable to have a little heating in reserve, to guard against the occasion periods of cold weather that can occur in the early part of the breeding season.

It should be emphasized however that too free a use of heating is unwise, and the aim should be to prevent any drop below freezing point rather than to provide unnaturally high temperatures. For this purpose the ideal heating system is thermostatically controlled. The setting should be quite low, say about 35 to 40 degrees Fahrenheit, which is quite adequate to prevent freezing of the water in winter and yet not too high to be unhealthy for the birds.

CAGES

Whatever may have been the final choice of accommodation for the housing of his canaries it is, of course, within the confines of cages that the birds will actually spend their lives, so that for the fancier these become the most important single item of his equipment.

Reference to some of the older standard works on canaries will frequently reveal a bewildering array of cages that were used by many fanciers in former times. These included stock cages, breeding cages, molting cages, show cages, nur-

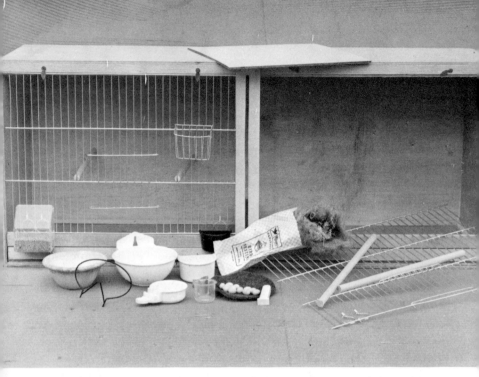

A double breeding cage with all its fittings and accessories used in breeding.

sery cages and bath cages but nowadays all but show cages, which are a specialized item, are usually combined in the form of a simple multi-purpose cage of well-proved design.

The word 'cage' is apt to conjure up an open wire structure similar perhaps to that in which pet birds are kept, but such designs are quite unsuitable for the serious breeder. The type known as a box cage is nowadays in almost universal use. As its name implies, it is of a box-shaped pattern with wooden sides, top, bottom and back, only the front being made of wire. It has every advantage to its credit, being easy to construct and maintain, and giving the birds a considerable degree of privacy, so valuable during the breeding season, with freedom from drafts and other external influences.

By varying its size the box cage can be made in any number of compartments separated usually by movable sliding partitions, and it is then accordingly designated a single, double or treble breeder. Each of these has its advantages but by far the most valuable as a multi-purpose unit is the double breeder, combining as it does reasonable size with ease in handling. As a stock cage it can accommodate two adult cock birds separated by the partition or three or four hens if open to its full length. During the breeding season it is ideal for housing a breeding pair and their young brood before weaning, and as a molting unit it can provide similar accommodation as when in use as a stock cage, or may be used for a small group of youngsters that are being molted together.

Cages can be purchased ready made from fanciers' suppliers but a good deal of pleasure, not to mention a saving of expense, can be obtained from making them oneself and they are quite within the capabilites of the average handyman. If the latter course is adopted the following points will prove useful.

Size: A suitable standard size is 36 inches long, 16 inches high and 12 inches deep but variations of an inch or so in either dimension would not matter, preference always being given to erring on the generous side especially if any of the larger breeds are being kept. It is important to keep to a standard pattern throughout one's stock as the cages will then be easily interchangeable if occasion arises, without upsetting the whole arrangement of the birdroom.

Design: There is obviously little variation possible in so simple a conception as the box cage but any temptation towards embellishment should be avoided and the pattern kept as simple as possible. The fewer odd pieces of woodwork the better from all points of view, and apart from the basic pieces which form the box, there is really only any necessity for one strip along the front to support the wires and one in the center at the bottom to carry the sliding partition. Cleaning trays to fit into the bottom of the cage can be made of wood or metal and should have just sufficient clearance to prevent them jamming.

Construction: 3/8-inch boards are generally used for all woodwork with the exception of the back which can be of plywood. Modern composition materials may be used with success but these should never be of a nature as would be liable to harbor insect pests. For the same reason the workmanship must be accurate, with close fitting joints which should be glued and nailed. All surfaces should be planed and sandpapered quite smooth to avoid any roughness that may provide lodgment for dirt or disease. Few fanciers nowadays make their own wire fronts as these can be quite cheaply bought in a variety of sizes ready to fit into any cage.

Finish: For many of the old-time fanciers the standard finish for the interior of their cages was whitewash but for their successors the modern latex paint has provided by far the most satisfactory cage decoration yet. This dries very quickly and is practically odorless—two points that render it far superior to gloss paints or enamels—so that an annual repainting is both simple and effective and can be carried out with a minimum of disturbance to the birds. The color chosen should preferably be a light one in order to keep the birdroom as bright as possible.

The exteriors of the cages can be similarly painted, but many fanciers prefer to use one or other of the proprietary wood preservatives or insect repellents both of which are entirely satisfactory.

An alternative to having separate cages, and one which can prove quite a saving of expense, is to construct a built-in cage system on similar lines to the built-in cupboards and other furniture frequently in use today. Fundamentally this would consist of a series of shelves 12 inches deep and 16 inches apart, which could then be partitioned at 36 inch intervals thus forming a basis for double breeders. All that would then be required would be the fixing of the wire cage fronts, the provision of a central carrier for the dividing slides and the addition of the cleaning trays. The birdroom itself would previously need to have been lined with plywood, hardboard or similar material which would thus form the backs of the cages.

Clearly such a system does not allow the complete removal of cages for any reason, such as repainting or disinfection, but it is quite easy to dismantle should the need arise, and with careful management and scrupulous attention to hygiene it can prove perfectly satisfactory.

CAGE FITTINGS

For whatever purpose the cage is being used, standard fitments in all cases will consist of the perches, seed hoppers and drinking vessels.

Perches: These can be purchased in convenient lengths from fanciers' suppliers or can be made at home. They should preferably be made of white softwood and should be of a variety of designs to allow some exercise to the birds' feet. They may be round, oval, square or rectangular in section, and should vary from about 3/8-inch to ¾-inch in width according to the age and type of bird being accommodated in the cages at the time.

As they need to be removed regularly for cleaning, the perches must never be made a permanent fixture. They are best fitted with a panel pin or small nail at the back, and a vertical notch at the front which will allow the former to be inserted into a small hole at the back of the cage, while the notch will fit firmly against an upright wire as the perch rests on the crossbar of the cage front. The length must be accurately adjusted so that the wire front does not bulge and yet does not allow the perch to drop down from its proper position. It is most important to ensure that they are quite firm, as various troubles are often attributable to unstable perches such as infertile eggs during the breeding season and lack of confidence and bad carriage, which may ruin a bird's chances on the showbench.

Some thought is necessary concerning the actual arrangement of the perches within the cages as regards height and spacing. Each single compartment should have two perches which must be so placed to give clearance to the bird's tail at the sides, some fanciers preferring them to be both at the same level and others favoring different heights. If the cage is being used at its double length, again two perches will usually be sufficient and this will allow the birds a little extra exercise in flying from end to end. Purchased cages sometimes are provided with a third perch running the length of the cage just in front of the feeding and water vessels, but this is quite unnecessary as it always gets soiled by droppings from the perches above and the birds can quite easily reach their food and water while standing on the floor.

It is a good plan to have plenty of spare perches so that clean sets are immediately available if needed at any time.

Seed Hoppers: In days gone by these were usually made of wood with a sloping glass front that could be removed for cleaning purposes, but they were eventually superseded by metal ones of similar design many of which are still used by established fanciers today. Far better in every respect however, are the modern transparent plastic hoppers now available which, with their smooth surfaces and rounded corners, are easy to clean and provide no lodgment for dust, dirt or insect pests.

Water Vessels: These are generally known to fanciers as 'drinkers', and are preferably of the open-topped glass variety, rounded inside, which are thus easily cleaned. Vessels with covered tops certainly prevent seed husks and dirt from falling into the water from cages above, but have the disadvantage of being less easy to clean. Drinkers made of other materials such as metal or plastic are rather less suitable as they are liable to become stained or corroded in course of time.

OTHER APPLIANCES

Fanciers of long standing tend to accumulate a great deal of equipment with the passing of time, much of which is useful and some of which is essential. For ordinary purposes the beginner will find that the following items are quite adequate and can be added to if and when he finds it is necessary.

(a) For Daily Use. *Grit Containers*, either small glass pots to stand upon the cage floor or metal tins to hook on to the inside of the cage front. *Cuttlefish Holders*, usually nothing more than a small clip to keep a piece of cuttlebone firmly in position. Although many fanciers merely wedge this substance between the wires it will eventually fall out as the birds wear it away. *Baths*, in the form of a special cage which hangs onto the cage front or a simple glass or earthenware dish that can be placed inside the cage. *Finger*

Drawers, which are slim plastic containers made to slip between the wires of the cage for the purpose of supplying small quantities of special seeds or foods.

(b) For the Birdroom. *Storage Bin*, either of wood or metal for the safe keeping of seeds and foods. These may be kept in separate cans, jars or bags inside the main container, according to the nature of the contents. *Cupboard*, for the storage of various items of equipment when not in use. Preferably this should have a working top which will then enable it to be used as a table. *Seed Sieve*, for the sifting and cleaning of seed. *Scraper and Small Brush*, for cage cleaning. *Broom and Dustpan*, for keeping the birdroom floor clean.

(c) For the Breeding Season. *Nesting Pans, Nest Pan Linings, Nesting Material Holders, Dummy Eggs, Egg Food Drawers, Feeding Trays, Mixing Basin* and *Spoon*. All these items will be discussed in greater detail in the section dealing with breeding.

As very many beginners commence their activities in the hobby with just two pairs of birds the following list of equipment is suggested as being the minimum requirements for two such pairs, along with a reasonable expectation of youngsters in the one year's breeding.

6 Double Cages
12 Seed Hoppers
12 Drinkers
36 Feet of Perching
12 Grit Containers
12 Cuttlefish Holders
12 Finger Drawers
6 Baths
6 Nesting Pans
6 Nest Linings
2 Nesting Material Racks
12 Dummy Eggs
6 Egg Food Drawers
6 Feeding Trays
1 Mixing Basin and Spoon
1 Seed Storage Bin
1 Seed Sieve

4
Feeding and General Management

In order to enjoy an active and healthy life the canary requires a properly balanced diet consisting of a number of complex food substances which are utilized by the body for a variety of purposes. The food that is eaten not only supplies heat and energy, and provides materials for growth and for the repair of tissues worn away as the result of normal day to day activity, but also gives protection against ill-health.

It will be apparent therefore, that the correct feeding of his stock is probably the most important single item to be considered by the fancier. Although his birds may be kept in an ideal environment, if the diet is in any way inadequate, failure, or at best only partial success, can be expected whereas, even under rather less than optimum housing conditions, if properly fed the birds will have a reasonable chance of doing well.

It is common practice to purchase correctly balanced seed mixtures and other special food preparations as marketed by birdfood specialists, but a knowledge of the underlying principles of feeding and the food values of the various seeds he is using can lead the fancier to a better understanding of the basic requirements of his charges.

TYPES OF FOOD

Foodstuffs are generally considered as consisting of six classes of substance namely, carbohydrates, fats and oils, proteins, mineral salts, vitamins and water, most of which are present in varying proportions in the different foods given to canaries.

Carbohydrates: The chief function of carbohydrates is to supply energy in a fairly quickly available form. Some are easily digested and are transported to the body tissues with little chemical change, others require a somewhat longer time to digest and undergo greater chemical changes before being absorbed, and still others are actually indigestible yet provide the necessary bulk or roughage in the diet. Among the foods commonly given to canaries in one form or another, sugars, which are present in fruit, milk or honey, are representative of the first class; starches which are found in canary seed, millet seed, oats, bread or biscuit meal, are typical of the second class, and celluloses, which are present in the cell walls of all plant material, are representative of the third. Nearly all seeds, even those of an oily nature, contain a large proportion of carbohydrates, so that seed eating birds like the canary are unlikely to suffer from any deficiency of this material.

Fats and Oils: These are sometimes also known as 'hydrocarbons' as they contain the same chemical elements as carbohydrates but in a much more complicated structural form. They yield about twice as much energy as the carbohydrates but undergo a much slower digestive process owing to the necessity of breaking down the complex fat molecules. Common sources of these foods for canaries include rape seed, niger seed, hemp seed, egg yolk and vegetable oils, but as birds seem not to require large amounts of fats, excessive feeding of these substances should be avoided.

Proteins: These are body building foods essential for growth and for the maintenance and repair of body tissues. They are particularly important in the diet during the breeding season, the hens requiring them for egg production and the young birds for rapid growth, and again during the molting season for the replacement of feathers which are entirely dependent upon protein. Most seeds contain between 14 per cent and 23 per cent of these substances, the oily seeds being generally the richer. Other sources for canaries include eggs, milk, dried yeast, whole meal and oatmeal. In seed eating birds, the majority of the protein intake will necessarily be of plant origin, but it is generally accepted that some animal protein is essential for the proper functioning of the system. In order to forestall any likelihood of deficiency many fanciers use feeding stuffs to which a high grade protein supplement has been added, during the critical periods of the year when it is most needed by the stock. Very little research work has been done on the scientific feeding of canaries but, in the case of poultry, it has been determined that the ratio of protein to carbohydrates and fats in the diet should be in the region of 1 to 4½.

Mineral Salts: Although needed in comparatively small quantities, certain mineral salts are vital to the body processes in a number of ways. The chief chemical elements required by birds are calcium, phosphorus, magnesium, potassium, iron, iodine, sodium, chlorine, manganese and sulphur; but these, fortunately, are usually present in the form of chemical salts in the normal diet supplied to canaries. If however any doubts are felt concerning possible mineral deficiency, supplements can be purchased either separately or ready mixed with the birds' supply of grit.

Vitamins: Like the mineral salts, vitamins also are needed in relatively small quantities and yet are essential for the proper functioning of the body, for if any of them are lacking, certain deficiency diseases may become apparent. Some vitamins are stored by the bird in the body tissues while others must be taken regularly, because any surplus in the diet is merely eliminated by excretion. The best safeguard against vitamin deficiency is a balanced diet which, in one form or another, contains such items as green vegetables, egg yolk, whole grain, milk, yeast, fish liver oil and wheat germ oil.

Water: In the strict sense water is not actually a food as it does not yield any energy, nor does it add any substance to the tissues of the body. It is nevertheless essential to the life processes in a number of ways and a large proportion of the body weight consists of water, which is largely organized into the protoplasm and intercellular spaces. It also provides the medium for transporting dissolved food substances from the digestive tract, via the bloodstream, to the cells of the body, and for the removal of waste materials through the kidneys. Some of the water requirements of the body are met by the food that is eaten, for even apparently dry, ripe seeds contain a certain percentage; but it is obviously mainly supplied in the form of drinking water.

FOODS FOR CANARIES

The earliest of writers ever to mention canaries, Conrad Gesner, also gave us the interesting fact that they were then fed on 'Line seed and Poppy seed and sometimes also Millet; but particularly they delight in sugar and the sugar cane, as also in that sort of Chickweed or Mouse-ear which they commonly call Henbit'. Although this was over 400 years ago the seeds listed, while not of great importance, still figure in mixtures given to canaries today, and every fancier will bear witness to the value of chickweed in the breeding room. Sugar, however, can hardly be classed as a major food item although canaries are undoubtedly fond of it.

Belonging as it does to the family Fringillidae, the canary is a finch and is primarily a seed-eating bird, so that this will always form the major part of its diet. The number of varieties of seed in general use is relatively small but quite adequate in feeding value if given in the right proportions.

Canary Seed: For most breeds of canary this is the main seed supplied and is the chief source of carbohydrates in the diet. Some fanciers prefer to have nothing else but plain canary seed in the hoppers, giving any others that may be required separately in the finger drawers. It is grown mostly in the Mediterranean countries or those with somewhat similar climates, such as Spain, Morocco, Turkey, Australia and Argentina, and lesser amounts are grown in Britain and the United States. This is now a commercial crop in the United States. The chief differences in the samples are in the size and degree of ripeness of the grain; but it is of course a well-known fact that the quality of the crop can vary according to the soil and climatic conditions in which it is grown, and for this reason many fanciers will purchase their canary seed from various sources and mix them together.

Rape Seed: This seed comes next in importance to canary seed, and in the case of the Roller canary actually supersedes it as the chief item in the diet. Being mainly of an oily nature it is frequently mixed with canary seed to provide a suitable staple mixture for the seed hoppers, generally in the proportion of three parts canary to one part rape, which produces an approximate ratio of 3:1:1 for the carbohydrates, oil and protein content. It cannot of course be guaranteed that any bird will actually consume the seed in the exact proportion that it is supplied in a mixture, and it is for this reason that some fanciers prefer to supply seeds separately.

Niger Seed: Having an almost identical analysis to rape seed, this is therefore of approximately equal feeding value. It is often used as a substitute for rape, especially by the breeders of Red Factor canaries, the reasons for which will be discussed in the chapter on that particular breed. Experienced breeders often affirm that niger is excellent for preventing egg binding in hens, and consequently it is commonly added to the diet from the New Year onwards, either as part of the staple mixture or as an extra in the finger drawers.

Hemp Seed: In general, this is the favorite seed of canaries, and they will usually pick out the hemp to eat first from any mixture that contains it. It is a very valuable food item but inclined to be rather stimulating, so that it is wise to supply it with discretion over the greater part of the year. Many fanciers however, use it freely during the breeding season, either crushed or soaked, without detrimental results. It is available commercially only in devitalized form; it is more commonly recognized under another name: Marijuana.

Teazle Seed: This seed was scarcely mentioned in the older manuals on canaries, but it is a firm favorite with the present-day breeder. It may form but a small part of a general dry seed mixture, but its chief value is in the breeding season when soaked teazle becomes one of the most important foods for the rearing of young canaries.

Maw Seed: This is the trade name given to the seed of the poppy. It is a very small, bluish-grey seed with a high oil content. It is relished by canaries almost as much as hemp, but is usually reserved for tonic or medicinal purposes, especially in cases of bowel trouble.

Linseed: Another seed with a high oil and protein content. This is frequently added to mixtures during the winter months and again during the molting season, when it is alleged to improve the sheen on the bird's plumage. In general however, canaries do not seem overfond of linseed and will eat very little of it from among a general mixture.

Oats: This grain is of some importance to breeders of Red Factor canaries, who may occasionally use it as a substitute for canary seed, and is sometimes used by others in small amounts during the winter months. It is said to be particularly useful in building up the frames of the larger breeds of canary during their growing period, but as its protein content is not appreciably different from other cereals, this is extremely doubtful. It is however, somewhat richer in oil than other 'mainly carbohydrate' seeds and may be of value on that account. It is generally supplied in the forms of hulled oats, clipped oats or pinhead oatmeal.

Condition Seed: This is a special mixture of several of the seeds already mentioned, plus a few more unusual ones such as dandelion, thistle, lettuce and gold of pleasure, and can be purchased ready mixed from most fanciers' seedsmen. As its name implies, it is used as a conditioner for show birds and breeding stock and is also given by many fanciers to all of their stock about once a week throughout the winter.

Wild Seeds: Keen fanciers who are conveniently situated near to open country will often go to the trouble of providing their birds with many of the wild seeds that are normally eaten by native finches. Although their nutritive value may not necessarily be high, they at least provide a welcome change from the usual dry seed mixture, and if given freshly gathered it is likely that their vitamin content will be better than that of stored seed. As the use of toxic sprays is a common practice in agriculture today, care should be taken that any wild plants offered to the birds have been collected from an uncontaminated source.

Greenstuff: Although its nutritive ratio is not great, fresh greenstuff forms an important part of the canary's diet mainly on account of its vitamin and mineral value. Most fanciers aim to provide some sort of greenstuff or its equivalent at least twice a week during the winter months, increasing it to every other day, or even daily, as the breeding season approaches. Items that may be offered include lettuce, watercress or mustard and cress, brussels sprouts, sprouting broccoli, kale, savoy cabbage, turnip tops, and wild plants known to be eaten by native finches. Care must be exercised in ensuring that all greenstuff is fresh and untainted and free from frost and, as an alternative if nothing green is available, a slice of sweet apple or some grated carrot will be appreciated.

Soft Food: This is a term applied to items of diet other than the seeds and greenstuff listed above. The commonest form of soft food is a kind of basic biscuit meal (cracker crumbs), to which hard boiled egg can be added to provide an important rearing food for young canaries. Many fanciers continue to feed a little of this substance perhaps once a week, and usually without the addition of the egg, throughout the winter. A number of branded soft foods of this nature are marketed by pet shops, many of them complete food in themselves containing as they often do such items as dried egg, powdered milk, wheat germ meal, dried yeast and various vitamin and mineral additives.

Another type of soft food favored by some fanciers is bread and milk, but as this has a decidedly laxative effect upon the birds it is preferably reserved for medicinal purposes.

Grit: It is of course a well-known fact that birds, because they have no teeth, require to swallow a small amount of grit as an aid to the digestion of their food, so that a supply of this should always be available in the cage. Various grits can be purchased but it is a common practice to provide a mixed article containing flint, sand and shell, with or without the addition of charcoal and mineral supplements.

Although it will by now be apparent that a great variety of foods can be given to canaries, it must not be assumed that every one of them *must* figure somewhere on the menu. Indeed, as with most varieties of livestock, it is generally true to say that the healthiest specimens are those that are kept upon a plain but wholesome diet rather than those that are constantly being offered tidbits and odds and ends of stimulating food.

Feeding by hard and fast rules can scarcely be recommended when dealing with living creatures. The experienced fancier keeps a watchful eye upon the condition of his stock

Analysis of feeding values of foods commonly given to canaries
(Compiled from various sources)

Substance	Proteins	Fats	Carbo-hydrates	Mineral Salts	Water
Canary Seed	13·5	5·5	52·0	7·0	15·0
Rape Seed	22·0	40·0	20·0	4·0	7·0
Niger Seed	21·5	41·0	21·0	3·0	11·5
Hemp Seed	16·0	31·5	23·0	6·0	11·0
Maw Seed	19·0	45·0	18·0	5·0	9·0
Linseed	23·5	35·5	22·0	4·0	9·5
Groats	15·0	9·0	67·0	2·0	6·0
Egg (Fresh Whole)	11·9	12·3	–	1·0	73·4
Egg (Dried Whole)	43·4	43·3	–	3·3	7·0
Biscuits (Plain Mixed)	7·3	11·2	73·3	1·0	5·2
Wholemeal Bread	8·2	2·0	47·1	1·9	40·0
Oatmeal	12·1	7·7	71·0	1·2	7·0
Milk (Fresh)	3·4	3·7	4·8	0·6	87·0
Milk (Dried Skimmed)	34·5	0·3	49·2	5·8	5·0
Watercress	2·9	Trace	0·7	0·9	91·1
Lettuce	1·1	Trace	1·8	0·3	95·2
Mustard and Cress	1·6	Trace	0·9	0·8	92·5
Brussels Sprouts	3·6	Trace	4·6	0·7	84·3
Savoy Cabbage	3·3	Trace	3·3	0·6	89·9
Carrot	0·7	Trace	5·4	0·5	89·8
Apple	0·3	Trace	11·7	0·2	84·5

The above figures should be taken as an approximate guide only, as they may well vary a little from sample to sample.

both collectively and as individuals and adjusts his feeding accordingly, but the beginner may feel in need of some guidance until he too can apply his judgement on these matters with confidence. For the assistance of such a beginner the following general feeding charts are suggested.

1. *Basic Winter Feeding:* Staple seed mixture for the seed hoppers—3 parts canary seed to 1 part red rape seed. The following daily additions to be given at the rate of one small teaspoonful per bird:

Sunday	Soft Food
Monday	Green Food
Tuesday	No extras
Wednesday	Condition Seed Mixture
Thursday	Green Food
Friday	No extras
Saturday	Niger Seed

2. *Beginning in the New Year:* Staple seed mixture for the seed hoppers—3 parts canary seed, ½ part red rape seed, ½ part niger seed. The following daily additions to be given:

Sunday	Soft Food
Monday	Green Food
Tuesday	No extras
Wednesday	Condition Seed Mixture
Thursday	Green Food
Friday	No extras
Saturday	Condition Seed Mixture

3. *Beginning in Early February:* Staple seed mixture as before, with the following daily additions:

Sunday	Soft Food
Monday	Green Food
Tuesday	No extras
Wednesday	Condition Seed Mixture
Thursday	Soft Food
Friday	Green Food
Saturday	Condition Seed Mixture

4. *Beginning in Early March:* Staple seed mixture as before with the following daily additions:

Sunday	Soft Food incorporating hard boiled egg
Monday	Green Food
Tuesday	Condition Seed Mixture
Wednesday	Green Food
Thursday	Soft Food and Condition Seed Mixture
Friday	Green Food
Saturday	Condition Seed Mixture

It will be found that under normal housing conditions canaries following the above regime will come naturally into breeding condition without unnecessary forcing. Details of feeding during the breeding and molting seasons will be given in the appropriate chapters.

MANAGEMENT

Among human beings there are some to whom cleanliness, tidiness and an orderly way of life comes as second nature, whereas others are permanently disorganized muddlers and often none too particular about the finer points of hygiene. Bird fanciers, representing as they do a fair cross-section of the general population, are to be found among both of these categories of person, and indeed among the many intermediate stages between, so that their birdrooms, reflecting their owners, may be anything from a model of efficiency to a slum. It goes almost without saying that although the birds themselves may have no particular aesthetic appreciation, they will certainly thrive better in a clean, tidy room under sound, regular routine than they will under conditions of haphazard management.

It should be the aim of every fancier therefore to work out for his own set of circumstances a program of jobs that will cover all eventualities over a period of time, and this should be deviated from only under exceptional conditions. Careful planning and regular attention are important aids to success, and become increasingly so the larger the number of birds that are kept.

General Organization: The evils inherent in overcrowding have already been pointed out, so that the caging of all stock should be directed with this in mind. It is a fairly general practice to cage adult cock birds singly as they are often inclined to fight, but this is by no means an invariable rule, especially during the winter months. However, with the approach of the breeding season fighting is much more likely. Hens generally agree much better and are usually kept in small groups which, if the double-cage system is being used, should not exceed four or five.

Exhibition birds will almost certainly need to be caged singly while the show season lasts in order to minimize the danger of soiling or damaging the plumage and to facilitate any special feeding that may be deemed necessary.

Some parts of the birdroom naturally tend to be brighter and more sunny than others, and frequently such spots are given to favorite birds. Other fanciers, believing in fair treatment for all, give their stock a move round every few weeks, and this has the additional useful effect of steadying the birds and making them accustomed to handling.

Daily Routine: The ordinary daily tasks in the birdroom are not especially demanding consisting as they do, except during special periods of the year, merely of feeding and watering the birds. Whether this should be done in the morning or the evening will largely depend upon the individual fancier but, if there is any choice in the matter, morning should be preferred, although many will also like to take an additional look round in the evening to ensure that all is well for the night.

The seed hoppers containing the staple mixture will need to have the loose husks blown from the surface and then should be filled up to normal level with similar seed. Water vessels will need to be emptied, wiped out with a clean cloth and then refilled with fresh water. This is a most important routine task which should never be neglected, and the lazy man's way of merely topping up the drinkers should never be countenanced. Stale, impure water is one of the most potent sources of trouble to all livestock, and the presence of green algae growing on the sides of the water vessels should be regarded as a disgrace.

If any extras in the way of feeding are needed such as greenstuff, softfood or special seeds these can also be attended to at this time, and the value of having a feeding chart pinned up in the birdroom for easy reference will become apparent especially if, as occasionally happens, some other member of the household is undertaking relief duty for the fancier.

Weekly Routine: The main weekly job for most fanciers is the cleaning out of the birds, which frequently extends over both days of the weekend when a large stock is involved. To be carried out effectively this needs to be done in an orderly way, and it is usually preceded by the baths.

Actually birds enjoy bathing at almost any time but undeniably they make quite a mess by splashing water about the birdroom so that unless one is prepared to clear up after them it is probably better to restrict this activity to immediately before the weekly cleaning out. Although it is helpful to have a fair number of baths available, it is not essential and a limited number hung onto the cages just in advance of one's cleaning operations is all that is needed. If any bird fails to make use of the bath in the time at its disposal there is no need to depart from routine for it will be found that some birds are in fact less frequent bathers than others.

To clean the cage is the next stage and here the double breeder pattern again proves its value, for it becomes a simple matter to run the occupants of the cage into one half, separating them by a sliding partition from the half being cleaned, and then to reverse the process for the opposite side. The most obvious need in cleaning is that of emptying the floor tray and refilling it with clean litter, and the question of what material is best to use for this purpose is one that will confront the beginner. Many of the older manuals recommend sand, and the floor trays often still retain the name of 'sand trays' from this era, but in a number of ways this substance is far from satisfactory. Even clean samples tend to stain the birds' plumage, and it is not sufficiently absorbent to keep the cage floor clean and dry, so that the birds' feet are a frequent source of trouble, becoming dirty with the accretion of droppings and grains of sand. Clean newspaper has been advocated by some fanciers but this quickly becomes fouled and needs changing daily to be effective, and in addition the printing ink invariably makes the birds' tails and feet dirty. Thick white blotting paper would be a better proposition but would probably prove too expensive.

Various other floor coverings have been tried but so far there is nothing that in any way equals white softwood sawdust for this purpose. It is clean, absorbent and deodorant having practically every advantage where other materials have drawbacks. One essential however, is that it must be of a coarse texture such as is produced by mortising, tenoning and similar types of woodworking machinery. The very fine floury sawdust is quite useless as it blows about with every movement of the bird, getting into food and water with detrimental results, especially to young stock.

Besides attending to the floor, the wire fronts should be detached so that the interior of the cage can be wiped out as it is sure to be fairly wet after the birds' bathing. The front itself should not be forgotten and must be wiped quite dry to discourage any rusting from setting in. If spare sets are kept, clean dry perches can now be inserted into the cages and the dirty ones set aside for washing in hot water to which a little disinfectant has been added. Care should be taken not to treat perches with strong antiseptic solutions for, in addition to the possibility of sore feet, sore eyes can result owing to the bird's habit of occasionally wiping its face on the perch.

During the cleaning of the cages a sharp lookout should be maintained for the presence of redmite, a parasite that makes its home in the cracks and crevices of woodwork and even at the ends of perches. Further details of this particular pest will be dealt with later.

After the cages themselves have been finished, the grit container will need cleaning out and replenishing and the next important job will then be sifting of the seed from the seed hoppers. The daily blowing of these merely removes a small surplus of husks from the surface, but during the week more tend to accumulate lower down among the seed, together with fragments of grit, particles of sawdust and other foreign matter. This can easily be removed in a small mesh kitchen sieve, and the hopper wiped clean before returning the sifted seed. Fanciers with larger stocks may wish to provide themselves with a larger sized sieve so that greater quantities of seed can be dealt with at one time, and some may even make use of small winnowing machines that can be obtained for the purpose.

Although the water vessels will probably appear perfectly clean if the daily wiping with a cloth has been strictly observed, it is still advisable to give them a thorough wash once a week in hot water to which a little antiseptic solution has been added, and this will ensure perfect hygiene and minimize any risk of waterborne infection. The same routine can, with advantage, be accorded any other feeding utensils that may have been in use during the week.

Spring Cleaning: Some weeks before the beginning of the breeding season the annual spring cleaning and overhaul of the birdroom and its equipment should take place, so that everything will be in perfect order before breeding commences. At this period the stock of birds is usually at its lowest, all the surplus having been disposed of and only the breeding pairs remaining, so that there will be plenty of spare cages to start work on and the birds can be transferred to these as the work progresses. A fine weekend in late February or early March is ideal for the purpose, so that a good deal of equipment can be taken outside the birdroom to allow the work to continue unhampered.

During spring cleaning each cage should be fully dealt with, removing it completely from the birdroom staging and giving it a thorough overhaul, disinfection and washing out. When dry the inside should receive a fresh coat of paint and the outside treated with creosote or similar wood preservative if considered necessary, care being taken to allow thorough drying and airing to minimize the smell before returning it to the birdroom. Any defects that may now be revealed must be made good, with particular attention being given to any points that may provide a hiding place for redmite.

The fabric of the birdroom itself should also be looked to at this stage, although it may not necessarily need redecorating every year. Fanciers should however take the opportunity of cleaning all parts that cannot be reached when the cages are in place, and it is useful to spray these areas with an insect repellent fluid such as can be purchased ready for use in an aerosol, or can be mixed oneself and used in a small hand spray but read cautionary statements on the label carefully; some products are not safe to use around livestock.

The life of any item of equipment can be greatly prolonged by careful treatment, and anything of only seasonal use, such as show cages and traveling cases, which by now will no longer be required, should be cleaned out, overhauled and repainted before being stored away until needed again. The same is true at the close of the breeding season, when many fanciers wisely have another partial 'spring clean' confining their attention to the cages that have been occupied by the breeding pairs, and to the special equipment that has been used and will not be required until the following year. It is far better to get these items cleaned, disinfected and put away, rather than to leave them lying about untidily for weeks with the intention of dealing with them later.

It will by now be appreciated that the management of livestock covers a wide range of activities, which in reality include housing and feeding as well as the various routine jobs referred to above. Some of these may perhaps tend to be of a rather monotonous nature, but the fancier who is prepared to give the necessary time and attention to small details will find that his trouble will be well repaid, for there is ample proof that success with canaries is very largely dependent upon the kind of treatment they receive.

5

Breeding — Practical

Apart from the small minority whose sole interest is in the exhibition field and who merely purchase their birds from practical breeders with this object in view, the great majority of fanciers regard the breeding season as being the focal point of the whole year's activities and it is certainly by far the most demanding in terms of time, skill and patience.

The conscientious canary breeder must be prepared to sacrifice much in the way of other leisure-time pursuits, for when breeding pairs are engaged upon rearing their young they require to be fed not less than three times daily, so that it is difficult to go far afield without making plans for returning in time to attend to the wants of the birds. In terms of skill, even when matters run a smooth course, situations are bound to occur which will need the exercise of sound judgement often involving some form of immediate action that could mean the difference between success and failure. Patience, of course, is a virtue that all livestock keepers must possess in abundance, and there is little doubt that many of the reasons for failure in canary breeding can be traced primarily to impatience on the part of the fancier.

The first of the problems in breeding that will have to be faced is that of deciding when to make a start, and inexperienced fanciers are often tempted to pair their birds far too early in the year—sometimes at such an unpromising time as February. The older canary manuals advised strongly against the rashness of such early breeding, for it must be appreciated that, although the days may be lengthening perceptibly, at the spring equinox there are still 12 hours of darkness which is too long a period for any newly hatched chicks to be without food.

It was stated in the preceding chapter that birds fed according to the recommended diet charts would come naturally into breeding condition at the right time without the use of any unduly stimulating foods. If an actual date is needed for guidance as to when this might be, it may be assumed that the latter half of March or the early part of April (early part of February in the U.S.) would be about right in most years. It has been proved experimentally that it is the lengthening hours of daylight that are responsible for stimulating the development of the sex glands in birds, weather conditions having but a slight modifying effect. The time when they reach the stage of readiness for breeding may vary from species to species but in the canary, kept in reasonable conditions and not subjected to periods of artificial lighting, this appears to be around the spring equinox, March 21.

The real criterion for the commencement of the breeding season however, and the only one that is heeded by experienced breeders, is not any particular date but the condition of the birds themselves. Nothing is to be gained if they are not yet ready, and equally no good will come of keeping them apart when they are in full breeding condition. To be able to discern just when the time is ripe is one of those matters of judgement that can only come with experience but, in general, the beginner may be guided by the following signs:

Cocks: These will already have been singing for many weeks but as they approach peak condition the intensity and volume of the song increases daily, and is usually accompanied by a swaying of the body from side to side with dropped wings and a restless 'marking time,' or moving along the perch as they sing. When not engaged in song they will frequently attempt to gain a view of any hens in nearby cages by putting their heads close to the wires or through the drinker holes, and yet another activity will be that of 'feeding' the perches. One of the phases of courtship in the canary is that of the cock feeding the hen and, in the absence of a mate, a cock that is ready for breeding will often deposit regurgitated food on the ends of the perches or even on his own feet.

Hens: These also will exhibit a general air of restlessness by flying ceaselessly from end to end of their cages or continuing to flap their wings even when stationary, and constantly calling to the cock birds. They will be observed carrying odd pieces of material about in their beaks and may begin to pluck their own feathers from the breast, flank or back. This habit should be discouraged by providing some sort of distraction such as a piece of string tied to the wires which they will enjoy trying to unravel. Some hens will start to form nests by making a depression in the sawdust in the corner of their cages, but the ultimate sign of readiness to breed is when they crouch low upon a perch with tail raised as though to invite coition whenever they hear the really ardent singing of a cock bird in a neighboring cage. When such a stage is reached no time should be lost in introducing the pair to each other.

BREEDING SYSTEMS

Various systems of breeding procedure have been evolved by canary fanciers in the course of years, all of which are in use in varying degrees today. The most widely used and the most natural of these methods is that of *single pairing* in which a cock and hen are mated at the beginning of the breeding season and remain together throughout its duration. This system is so popular because it is in general the easiest form of management and the one that is least likely to present any special difficulties. For this reason it is the one to be recommended for the beginner.

Also in fairly common use is the system of *double pairing* in which each cock bird is mated with two hens for the season, the advantage of which is a saving of space since fewer cocks are needed in relation to the total number of birds kept. This method of breeding can be accomplished in one of two ways; in the first, the cock is mated with one hen and, after putting her safely to nest, is then transferred to his second mate. When she too is safely incubating her clutch of eggs he is returned to the first hen in time to help rear the brood and to put her to nest for the second time. Finally he is placed with the second hen once again for the same purpose.

The second way of operating the double pairing system is to allow the cock bird to put both of the hens to nest simultaneously, to which end he is allowed to run with each of his partners alternately for a portion of each day, transferring him from one to the other morning and evening.

A further system is that of *multiple pairing* in which a single cock bird is mated to any number of hens during the course of the season. This method is mainly used by the advanced breeder who may be line breeding, test mating, or progeny testing, and has its parallel in the stud methods of other livestock. As each hen becomes ripe for breeding the cock bird is introduced to her for a brief period only to allow coition to take place and is then returned to his stock cage. It is usual to repeat the process daily until the hen has laid her clutch of eggs, as it is by no means certain that a single act of coition will result in complete fertilization. Under this system the cock bird plays no further part and the rearing of the young birds is the sole responsibility of the hen.

GENERAL PRECEPTS IN BREEDING

Apart from the occasions when he may be working upon some specialized objective, such as the establishment or intensification of some particular show point, it may be assumed that the aim of the breeder of exhibition canaries is to produce birds of a high general level of excellence, most of which will measure up to the breed standard with a fair degree of accuracy. To achieve this he must be able to select from among his stock those breeding pairs which are most likely to give the desired results, and this he does by reference both to the visible qualities of each bird and to its recorded pedigree.

The beginner will of necessity be limited to visual selection only, until he has been in operation long enough to have accumulated sufficient background knowledge to assist him in the pairing of the birds, and it will be appreciated that it is essential for him to have a clear understanding of the basic show points of his own particular breed together with a mental picture of what the ideal should look like, and to make his selection with these in mind. Every breeder, whether he may be conscious of it or not, is exercising his critical faculties when selecting his birds for breeding and it is obvious that the higher his standards are the better will be the ultimate quality of his stock.

It is advisable to be really discriminating in one's approach and to be quite ruthless in rejecting unsuitable material, for it is always preferable to have a few good pairs for breeding rather than many mediocre ones.

To tackle the job in a practical manner, the novice should first make a rigorous selection from among his stock on the grounds of health and vigor and no birds should be accepted that fail in either of these respects, however desirable they may otherwise seem. Secondly, a visual standard should be applied and any birds with *serious* faults rejected at once, as these are far easier to perpetuate than to eradicate. In the nature of things there are very few perfect birds about so that minor faults may have to be overlooked for the moment, presenting the breeder with a challenge to his skill in trying to eliminate them. Finally, reference should be made to the pedigree to ensure that in all other respects the bird may have a history that makes it worth breeding from; too many fanciers have, to their regret, retained a bird for breeding 'because its great-great-grandfather was a National winner,' and overlooked the fact that there has not been another winner of note in the family since!

In order to improve one's stock and to produce the best possible youngsters, the usual procedure is to mate the best cock bird in the stud with the best hen, provided that circumstances such as color and relationship will permit. The second best pair should similarly be matched up, then the third, and so on throughout the stock, and by systematically carrying out this method of pairing in conjunction with the lines of selection already indicated, a high standard should not be difficult to maintain.

BASIC MATINGS

(I) The orthodox mating in normal yellow ground canaries is yellow x buff, and it makes no difference which bird of the pair is the yellow and which is the buff. It may be a yellow cock mated to a buff hen, or a buff cock mated to a yellow hen, and in either case the result will be the same—approximately 50 per cent of each color among the youngsters. There is no sex-linkage between these two color types and cocks and hens may be produced indifferently in each.

(II) Where dominant white ground canaries are being bred, the correct basic mating is white ground x normal yellow ground, and again, there being no sex-linkage involved, the parent birds may be of either color and in the case of the normal parent it may equally well be either yellow or buff. The youngsters resulting from this mating will be 50 per cent white and 50 per cent normal. Nothing is to be gained from mating dominant white x dominant white as no greater number of white youngsters will be produced, and in addition, owing to the involvement of a lethal factor, 25 per cent of the chicks from the mating are non-viable.

(III) In the case of the crested breeds of canary, these are invariably mated as crest x plainhead and, following the lines of the two previous examples, 50 per cent crested and 50 per cent plainhead youngsters are the normal expectation. These three matings are typical of the heterozygous dominant x homozygous recessive Mendelian mode of inheritance and, together with the sex-linked cinnamon inheritance they will be explained in terms of the genetics involved in the next chapter.

BREEDING SEASON ACCESSORIES

Brief mention has already been made in an earlier chapter of the items of equipment that are considered essential for the breeding season, and somewhat fuller details of them are now necessary.

Nest Pans: In the confines of a plain breeding cage where there are obviously no natural nesting sites, provision is made for the canary to build a nest by supplying a nest pan. These can be purchased from fanciers' suppliers and are generally made of metal, earthenware, or plastic, although special small wickerwork baskets are favored by some breeders. In either case they are supplied complete with wire holders for hanging them onto the back of the cage where a small hook

Three types of nesting receptacle, an earthenware pan with wire holder, a plastic pan, and an old-fashioned, though still useful, nest box.

for the purpose should be provided. As an alternative, simple nest boxes can easily be constructed from wood and perforated zinc and are preferred by some fanciers.

Nest Linings: Over years of domestication many canary hens seem to have lost some of the art of nest building, so that in order to give adequate protection to the eggs and young birds it is usual to provide the nest pans with felt linings. They can be purchased cheaply, blocked to shape all ready for fixing inside the pan, but the fancier who may wish to save this small expense would no doubt be able to devise a suitable substitute—many for example could be cut from a spare piece of carpeting underfelt.

Nesting Material: This item too is supplied very cheaply by pet shops in conveniently sized bundles, cleaned and sterilized ready for use, but the fancier who wishes to provide his own should use fine hay and moss with cow-hair or similar material for the lining, all of which should receive some form of sterilizing treatment before use, such as heating in an oven or immersion in a disinfectant solution.

Nesting Material Racks: These are small wire holders into which the nesting material can be placed and hung for convenience onto the cage front so that the birds can help themselves.

Dummy Eggs and Egg Box: It is an almost universal practice to remove the canary's eggs as they are laid and to substitute dummies until she is ready for incubation. These too can be very cheaply bought from the appropriate source and are usually made of plastic, earthenware or wood. An egg box suitable for holding the real eggs should be constructed and provided with compartments corresponding to the number of breeding cages in the room, each compartment being lined with some soft material such as cotton wool to guard against any possibility of damage.

Egg Food Drawers: These are earthenware or plastic containers, rather on the lines of the finger drawers previously described. They are however, much larger and are made to fit securely under the cage door, for which purpose appropriate grooves are incorporated into the design. Various patterns are on the market but the circular ones are to be preferred, as there are then no awkward corners in which stale particles of food may become lodged.

Feeding Trays: These are among the most useful pieces of equipment in the breeding room. They are larger versions of the egg food drawer, measuring 6 inches by 4½ inches, and are made of wood. They will hold two egg food drawers side by side which is very useful when different items of food are being offered, but their particular value is for the feeding of newly weaned youngsters who will often take more readily to feeding from the trays rather than from other receptacles.

Mixing Basins, etc.: Various items of general kitchen equipment are necessary for preparing different types of food. Apart from the obvious necessity of mixing bowls and spoons, several jam jars for soaking seed and a sieve for straining should be provided, and doubtless other useful items will find their way from kitchen to birdroom as time goes on!

Breeding Room Register: It is essential for the serious breeder to keep accurate details of all that he does, and for this purpose the *Breeding Room Register* provides a practical way of recording the daily activities in the birdroom. Entries concerning pairing, laying, dates of hatching, weaning and so on should be made, the essentials later to be transferred to a properly kept Stock Book, Pedigree Register or Card Index File, whichever system may be favored. The Breeding Room Register need be nothing more elaborate than a child's exercise book ruled up according to the fancier's own ideas of record keeping.

PAIRING

In readiness for the start of the season, the hens should preferably be all ready and in their breeding cages for at least a fortnight before the anticipated time of mating, in order to allow them to become quite steady and fully accustomed to their quarters. Before transferring them they should have their claws examined, and if they appear to be too long they should be trimmed with a sharp pair of nail scissors, care being taken not to cut too close to the blood vessel which runs for a portion of the length of the nail. This can easily be seen in a good light, but is rather more difficult to discern in birds with dark colored toe nails.

In the case of heavily feathered breeds it is often the practice to trim the feathers around the vent and beneath the tail, making them somewhat shorter, since the presence of long and dense feathering may prove a material barrier to successful fertilization. At the same time similar treatment should be given to the toenails and vent feathers of the cock birds, which may then be returned to their stock cages pending mating time or, if single pairing is being practiced, they may be placed in the opposite compartments of the breeding cages to their partners with the wooden sliding partition between.

As the birds become obviously ready for mating, a wire slide may be substituted and the birds' reactions to their first sight of each other noted. If the hen immediately invites coition there is no point in delaying matters any further, but otherwise a day or so may be allowed to elapse before the final withdrawal of the slide which will permit the birds complete access to each other.

The attitude of a newly introduced pair can vary considerably and sometimes bickering will take place, but unless this continues for a length of time or reaches serious proportions there is no need for alarm, nor is there any reason to separate the pair until they may be better disposed towards each other.

Trimming toenails—a routine matter that may need attending to once or twice a year.

Example of entry in Stock Book or Card Index File:

RING NO: Red 23   SEX AND COLOUR: Cock. Clear Yellow.

○   HATCHED: 23.4.66   HOW BRED: Orange 16 × Blue 31

DESCRIPTION: Good type all round. Especially good head. Fails a little in wing carriage. Excellent colour and feather.

SHOW RESULTS: 1966—Southampton 3rd out of 8 (Judge — A. Brown). Manchester 4th out of 10 (Judge — B. Jones). National 6th out of 17 (Judge — C. Smith).

○   BREEDING RESULTS: 1967—Fertilized all eggs (12). Left with hen throughout. Proved reliable feeder.

REMARKS: Sold to D. Robinson 16.11.67.

On reverse side details of Pedigree:

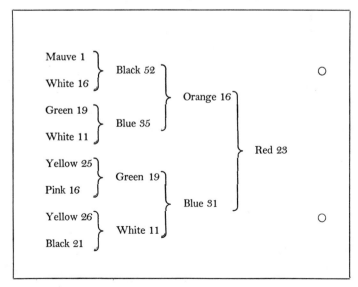

NEST BUILDING

A day or two after pairing, the nest pan complete with its lining should be hung onto the small hook at the back of the cage. The exact placing is relatively of little importance, but the most widely accepted position is perhaps midway between the two perches and with the rim at about 1½ to 2 inches above their level. The felt lining is often secured to the pan by means of paste or similar adhesive, but this makes it rather a messy business to remove at a later date when preparing the nest pan for another lining. A better method is to sew it firmly into position with a strong thread using the ventilation holes at the sides and bottom of the pan for the pur-

A well-matched pair of Gloster Fancy canaries at their nest.

pose. Some fanciers previously dust the underside of the felt with insect powder or give a quick lick of creosote, paraffin or other insect repellent to the inside of the pan before fixing the felt.

Nesting material in the special holder can also be supplied at this time, but it is advisable to limit the quantity at first as there is often a period of 'playing about' at nesting before the hen really settles to do the job, during which time the material gets thoroughly dirty. When it can be seen that she is in earnest, the material can be supplied as fast as she is inclined to use it until the nest has been completed. As has been previously pointed out, many hens are slovenly nest builders so that sometimes fanciers will assist them by roughly molding the shape of the nest for them when it can be seen that help is needed. Most hens will accept this with indifference while some will only throw it all out again, having no use for anything but their own efforts, poor though these may be!

EGG LAYING

If the breeding pairs are in full condition at the time of mating, the first egg of the clutch may be expected within a week. Various signs indicating the approaching event may be observed, including the hen roosting close to the nest or even inside it at night, an increased consumption of water during the period of about 48 hours before the commencement of laying and, in particular, the hen appearing rather less active and somewhat 'heavy-looking' in the evening, before an egg is due. When such signs are in evidence, the fancier should be on the lookout for the first egg, which normally is laid in the early morning, generally before 7:30 a.m., so that fanciers who attend early to their duties in the birdroom may often see hens in the act of laying. It is not altogether wise to disturb them too early during this critical period however, owing to the nervousness of some hens.

When the first egg has made its due appearance it should be removed from the nest to the prepared place in the egg box and a dummy substituted, awaiting an opportune moment when the hen leaves the nest for feeding. Eggs are best handled by means of a teaspoon, even for those who have a delicate sense of touch and ample confidence in the matter, for it is always better to avoid any possibility of an accident. The normal frequency of laying in the canary is once every 24 hours, so that each succeeding morning the eggs should be removed as laid until the fourth has made its appearance, when they can all be replaced and the hen 'set' for her period of incubation. The reason for this simple practice is to ensure that the whole of the clutch will hatch at about the same time and the chicks will thus all have an equal start in life.

It is during the period of egg laying that the fancier may be unfortunate enough to experience the first of the difficulties that can confront a canary breeder—that of egg bind-

Gloster Fancy hen (a green) incubating.

ing. Let it be said at once however, that given sound, healthy stock that has been properly fed and managed throughout the winter such an eventuality is unlikely, and it is mainly in weakly birds, or those that may be overfat or in soft condition—in short, it is with birds that should not have been bred from at all, that difficulties may well occur. The trouble arises at the time of parturition when, for one of the reasons just mentioned, the hen is unable to pass the egg, causing her anything from mild distress to complete prostration according to the severity of the problem.

The symptoms of egg-binding are easily recognized. The hen may be found in the nest or upon the floor of the cage with feathers all puffed up, eyes half closed and with an utterly 'miserable' look about her. She may make periodic efforts to expel the egg, but these generally are unsuccessful and leave her in a state of weakness. The best form of treatment is to remove the hen to a really warm place and it will often be found that in an hour or so this in itself may be sufficient to bring relief. If thought necessary, a very small amount of warm olive oil can be dropped into the vent to act as a lubricant to ease the passage of the egg, but no attempt should be made to extract it manually as this will almost always cause breakage and internal injury to the bird.

INCUBATION

Before returning the clutch of eggs to the nest it is advisable, with as little fuss as possible, to clean out the cage so that the hen will not be subjected to any further disturbance while setting. A note of the date should also be made in order that the expected time of hatching can be calculated. The period of incubation in the canary is 13 or 14 days, depending to some extent upon the closeness with which individual hens brood their eggs, and it is therefore wise to be prepared for the event on the thirteenth day although it need cause no anxiety if hatching has not taken place by then.

During this period it is usual to feed the birds upon a plainer diet than hitherto, and a staple mixture of 3 parts canary seed to 1 part rape seed in the seed hoppers, with a little greenfood given twice weekly, should be sufficient in

Gloster Fancy hen with her chicks only a few days old.

most cases. If single pairing is being employed, this will be a time of relative inactivity for the cock bird and occasionally some are to be found who will make themselves a nuisance by worrying the hen or interfering with the nest. If such should prove to be the case, the sliding partition can again be brought into use to remove him from temptation and to allow the hen to complete her incubation in peace.

HATCHING

On the day before the eggs are due some fanciers provide the hen with a bath, holding the view that a degree of moisture is a necessary aid to hatching. Not all hens will make use of it however, and they normally hatch just as well without. A little egg food may be supplied at this time to give the pair a preliminary taste of one of the main rearing foods that they will be using, and on the morning when hatching is due this can be provided again.

If all goes well, the signs that hatching has occurred may well be the appearance of empty egg shells on the floor of the cage and the faint but quite audible cheeping of the newly emerged chicks; but if nothing is noted the beginner should avoid disturbing the hen through anxiety to ascertain if she has any young ones, as it is nothing unusual for the eggs to be a day late in hatching. However, if the eggs become more than 48 hours overdue it is almost certain that the second of the season's disappointments will be in store for the breeder in the shape of infertile eggs or "dead-in-shell"

Gloster Fancy hen with chicks now about a week old.

chicks. In either case there is no remedy, and the breeding pair should be given a brief period of reconditioning before being mated again in about ten days' to a fortnight's time.

REARING

Like other nidicolous birds, the young canary is entirely dependent upon its parents for the first few weeks of its life and they supply all of its wants until it is weaned at the age of 21 days. The fact that some perform their duties well, some indifferently, and others not at all leaves the breeder very much at the mercy of fate, but it is fortunate that by far the larger proportion belong to the first category, and that really bad parents may be considered a rarity. In the past, breeders of exhibition stock made wide use of common canaries as foster parents, or 'feeders' as they were called, in the mistaken belief that it was too much of a strain upon their highly-bred hens to rear their own young. Over a period of years this probably led to a weakening of the parental instinct in the exhibition birds and, with selection being made purely upon show points, strains were being produced that were poor feeders. Nowadays wiser action is usually taken, and in most breeds of canary strains of unsatisfactory breeders have largely been eliminated.

A great number of methods for the rearing of young canaries are in operation, although it may be said that they are mainly in the nature of variations upon a few basic principles. Almost every fancier seems to have his own special version, but it is remarkable how one man will succeed and another fail while using methods that in all particulars seem to be identical. There are some of an experimental turn of mind who will try out something new almost every season, getting much pleasure and learning a good deal in the process, but it is perhaps more general for a fancier, after a year or so of trial and error, to settle upon a system that he finds successful and to keep to it.

Basically, the foods employed in rearing consist of soft food, soaked seeds, wild seeds and greenstuff, and it is mainly in matters of detail concerning quantity, methods of preparation, and at what stage of rearing they should be given or withheld, that fanciers may differ.

It has already been explained in the preceding chapter that soft food is an important rearing medium for young canaries, and that a number of brands of this substance are marketed under various trade names by pet shops. Some of them are complete rearing foods in themselves and only need preparing according to the makers' directions before feeding to the birds, so that they provide the perfect answer for the busy fancier or for one who is not inclined to dabble in avian dietetics. Others are definitely low in protein content and state that they need the addition of hard boiled egg to make good this deficiency. This is not difficult to do, for, after boiling for about ten minutes, the egg (both yolk and white) can easily be pressed through a small-meshed kitchen sieve with a wooden spoon and can then be readily incorporated with the soft food, at the rate of about one egg to one breakfast cupful of soft food.

For any fancier who may wish to make his own rearing food the recipes are many, but the following suggestion, which is a slight variation on one given by C.A. House in his book *Canaries* (1923), will usually be found to give good results if mixed with egg in the manner just described:

> Wholemeal bread 10 parts, fine oatmeal 5 parts, and 1 part of sugar, Maw seed and any proprietary baby cereal food. The bread should first be cut into slices and dried in a slow oven before being finely ground up through a domestic mincer. It can then be thoroughly mixed with the other ingredients and stored in any suitable container until required for use. Like most other soft foods it will need to be slightly moistened before feeding to the birds, but should never be made wet or sloppy—the correct traditional description being 'crumbly moist'.

The most suitable mixture of seeds for soaking consists of rape, teazle and hemp, in equal proportions or with a double amount of teazle if desired. The object of soaking is to soften the hard dry cotyledons of the seed to make them more suitable for young birds, and to this end 48 hours' immersion is generally sufficient. To ensure a constant daily supply, two containers such as large jam jars will have to be used in rotation, and each morning the seed that has been soaking for 48 hours will need straining and drying slightly in a cloth before feeding to the birds, while that which has only been soaking for 24 hours will need a thorough rinsing under a tap before being returned to the jar and covered again with clean water. In an emergency, if soaking has been forgotten, the same result can be achieved by boiling the seed, bringing it quickly to the boil and then allowing it to simmer for about twenty minutes.

Wild seeds employed by canary breeders are those that are commonly consumed by our native finches in rearing their young, and if plenty are available they can be supplied almost at will. It is emphasized that it is the seeding part of the plant that is required and not the green leaves, and it will be found that canaries are particularly fond of the semi-ripe, whitish seeds of chickweed and have been known to rear their broods almost entirely upon this one item.

Suitable greenstuff that may be offered to the breeding pairs during the spring and early summer months is fairly limited in variety, and probably the best will be garden-grown lettuce which can be given fresh and crisp in which state it will be readily appreciated by the birds.

Today's fancier has one great advantage over his predecessors in that he has at his disposal the domestic refrigerator. During the summer months egg food and soaked seed tend to deteriorate and become sour fairly rapidly so that it was necessary, in the past, to prepare each item afresh three or four times daily. Nowadays a sufficient quantity for the whole day can be mixed in the morning and kept in the fridge until required for use. When feeding pairs of canaries with young broods the rule should be 'a little, and as often as possible,' but with the majority of breeders this will usually resolve itself into three times daily: morning, midday and early evening, but if extra feeds can be arranged so much the better. At each feeding, any unconsumed food left from the previous supply should be removed entirely and a fresh quantity provided *in clean vessels*. In this way no stale or souring items can possibly be available, thus avoiding any risk of internal disorders among the birds.

It has already been stated that the actual details of feeding may vary from fancier to fancier, but for any newcomer in need of some guidance in the matter the following system which represents a reasonably middle course should prove helpful:

For the first two days after hatching, egg food only should be given, but on the third day a little greenfood can also be offered. On the fourth day a small spray of half-ripe wild seed, such as chickweed, can be added, and on the fifth day the soaked seeds, so that from then onwards all items can be made available from which the parent birds can make their choice.

Quantities will have to be adjusted by observation according to how much is being taken, and it will probably be noted that the birds are highly individualistic in their taste, some pairs preferring certain items to the exclusion of others, while other pairs will take all that is offered indiscriminately.

A watchful eye must at all times be kept upon the progress of the chicks, as there are various troubles that might possibly occur during the time that they are in the nestling stage. They are briefly listed here:

1. *Falling from the nest.* This may happen when they are very tiny and is usually due to carelessness on the part of the hen when leaving the nest. It is remarkable that they will generally survive such an accident if discovered in time, and even a cold and apparently lifeless chick if warmed in the hand will soon revive and may then be returned to the nest.

2. *Sweating.* As birds are in fact unable to sweat this term is something of a misnomer, but it is still used by fanciers if the chicks, instead of looking clean and fluffy, appear damp and messy. Until the young birds are able to defecate over the edge of the nest pan it is the practice of the hen to keep the nest clean by swallowing their droppings which are enveloped in a gelatinous sac, but if, through incorrect feeding or more particularly through allowing food to become sour, diarrhea is induced, this becomes an

impossibility. This misfortune obviously is one which can be avoided with proper care, but if it does occur the remedy is to provide a clean nest, pay scrupulous attention to the feeding and incorporate a little powdered arrowroot in the egg food until the trouble disappears.

3. *Non-Feeding.* If the chicks are making no progress and seem to have little food in their crops it may be concluded that the parents are bad feeders. This is an unfortunate occurrence, and little can be done apart from fostering out the youngsters to pairs that are feeding well and have chicks at about the same stage of development. It *is* possible to hand-rear young canaries but the demands made upon time and patience are so considerable that for most people it becomes an unenviable task.

Given good healthy breeding stock however, and under sound management, troubles are rarely encountered and the nestlings continue to thrive without a check right up to the time when they are ready to leave the nest. At about five or six days old the first signs of feather quills can be discerned; at a week their eyes are opening and at ten days the feather tracts can be clearly traced. The feathers are expanding nicely from their quills at twelve days old and at a fortnight the chicks may appear to be quite fully clothed as far as their backs are concerned. It will be found however, that the feathers underneath have not expanded sufficiently to cover the breast bone and it will be another four or five days before they are completely fledged.

WEANING

The exact age for separating them from their parents will vary to some extent according to how well the youngsters have been reared, but on an average it will be at about 21 days old. For a day or two previous to this the bolder ones among them will in all probability have been hopping about on the edge of the nest, or even leaving it for the perches or to explore the floor of the cage, and when they are observed pecking about inquisitively it is usually a good time to take the decision to wean them.

This is best accomplished in the morning, for they will then have all day to become familiar with their new quarters and to learn to feed themselves. If however, it becomes obvious that they are hungry, they can be returned to their parents in the late afternoon and another attempt made to render them independent on the following day. It is easy to distinguish the chicks that are not feeding themselves for they have a 'miserable' look, and repeatedly utter a plaintive and penetrating chirp—often while standing on the feeding tray and actually watching the others tucking into the rations!

There should be no immediate change in the food that is offered to the newly-weaned youngsters, the egg food, soaked seed, seeding chickweed and greenstuff still being supplied three times daily. The value of the feeding tray at this stage is incalculable, as the various foods can be scattered upon it and several chicks can perch around it at the same time in a way that seems to be mutually beneficial. It is most important to avoid any stale food being left about in the cage during this period, and to this end it is preferable to have paper upon the floor which can quickly be removed morning and evening and the cage thus kept in a hygienic condition.

RINGING

It is imperative for the serious canary breeder to place identification rings upon the legs of his birds, and this can be accomplished in one of two ways. One is to use 'split' rings, which are easily put on to the young ones as they are transferred from their parents at weaning time. They are lightweight colored plastic rings, numbered consecutively, which can be opened by a special expanding tool and then slipped over the shank of the bird's leg. Holding the ring in position, the tool can then be withdrawn leaving the ring encircling the leg. The other method is to use closed rings and these can only be put on when the chicks are quite small—usually at about five or six days old. The front three toes are first brought close together and the ring is passed over them, then back over the ball of the foot and finally along the shank of the leg, to which the rear toe has been temporarily pressed until the ring is clear of the toenail, when it can be allowed to resume its natural position. This is not a difficult task, but some breeders object to its use mainly on the grounds of the early disturbance of the nest, and because *occasionally* a hen will take exception to the rings and try to remove them, usually with injurious results to the chicks.

SECOND BROODS

Although everything so far may have the appearance of being reasonably straightforward and without any insuperable difficulties, the starting of a second nest by the breeding pair may present some minor complications which will need a little care in handling. The urge to nest again is sometimes delayed until the young of the first brood are weaned, in which case no problem of management arises; but frequently the hen is ready to lay again some days before the first chicks are able to leave the nest. Evidence of this will become clear when she is observed trying to remake the old nest, often shuffling down among the youngsters with the result that sometimes an unfortunate chick is ousted in the process. Some hens, in their desire for fresh nesting material, will commence to pluck the feathers of their first brood, and this will obviously be detrimental to their progress. In the case of Lizard canaries where perfection of plumage is essential, it must be avoided at all costs as it will ruin their chances as show birds.

The wise fancier will therefore be prepared for the second nesting cycle by providing a newly lined pan in the opposite compartment of the cage and building material sufficient for the hen's needs. Even so, complications may yet arise, as for instance when the hen still insists on occupying the old nesting site, in which case it must be the chicks that are transferred to the new position. In between building a new nest and laying a fresh clutch of eggs the hen will continue to feed the first brood, but once she has started to incubate it will be left entirely to the cock bird, so that if at this stage the youngsters are still not ready for weaning it may become advisable to separate them by a wire slide from the hen, who will then be able to settle down to her duties without interference.

Many fanciers allow their birds to carry on for a third 'round' of nests, but the advisability of this practice is open to question and must be determined by circumstances. If two really good rounds have already been produced, any further breeding may be considered unnecessary, but on the other hand if results on the first two rounds have been poor and it is not too late in the season, a third nest may be justified. It will often be found in practice however, that third nests are rarely worth while, probably owing to the lower vitality of the breeding stock later in the season. A poor start is not often redeemed by later successes and late hatched chicks never seem to thrive to the same degree, often running into molting difficulties late in the autumn.

CARE OF YOUNG STOCK

The post-weaning period is no less critical for young canaries than that spent in the nest, and it must not be imagined that because they are safely away from their parents and feeding themselves satisfactorily that they will automatically be reared to maturity. Given proper care and attention there should be no losses beyond this stage, but it is unfortunately true to say that many young canaries *are* lost, although this can almost always be traced to errors on the part of the owner. Primarily, it must not be forgotten that even though they may appear quite large and robust and that, at the age of eight weeks, are not much inferior in size to adult birds, they are still babies.

The young birds must have ample room for development and to this end they must never be overcrowded, four or five to a double-compartment cage being the limit. It has already been recommended that paper on the floor, changed at least daily, is the ideal way of preventing any stale food from remaining in the cage, and this should be maintained up to the age of at least eight weeks. Although it may entail extra work it is well worth while, as the delicate internal organs are more susceptible to digestive and intestinal disorders than those of adult birds, and anything that may possibly cause trouble in these directions should be avoided.

Similarly, the hard dry seeds that adult digestions are capable of dealing with must not enter too soon into the diet of the youngsters, and one of the commonest causes of loss is through allowing them unlimited access to this item too early in their careers. Any sudden changes of food, in fact, should always be avoided and the egg food, soaked seeds, seeding weeds and grasses, plus a little fresh lettuce daily, should continue as before. Some fanciers, owing to a fear of septic bacilli which multiply very rapidly in humid summer weather, cease to add egg to the soft food and rely upon some other form of protein supplement, but under hygienic conditions and with frequent changes of food no trouble from this source need be encountered.

The first hard seed should not be introduced before the youngsters are six weeks old, and then should only be in the form of a few grains sprinkled over the other food on the feeding tray. The amount can gradually be increased during the next fortnight until at the age of eight weeks the normal seed hoppers can be hung upon the cages for a few hours daily; but even then the supply of other foods should still be available right up to the commencement of the molt.

During this period of the young birds' life, the fancier can take various steps towards the final goal of the show-bench. Careful watch must be kept at all times for any signs of feather plucking among the youngsters, and if any offender is detected he should be separated from the remainder before the vice spreads. Attention can often be diverted, as in the case of an over-forward hen, by means of a piece of string attached to the wires of the cage. Early familiarity with a show cage is a great advantage, and to this end training can begin when the youngsters are four or five weeks old by hanging a show cage onto the front of their stock cage, with the two doors open to allow them free access. Young birds being of an inquisitive nature soon find their way into the show cage, and eventually take great delight in hopping in and out of it all day long. They learn quickly, and after a week or so can readily be taught to enter the cage at will by guiding them in gently with a training stick. With patience it will soon be possible to handle the cage with the young birds inside, until its confidence is established and no uneasiness is apparent at being isolated inside the smaller cage.

6
Breeding — Theory

Having in some measure mastered the purely practical aspects of breeding procedure, the serious fancier will probably wish to learn something of the underlying reasons accounting for some of his results. In doing so he will find that however unusual these may at first appear, they are all, in fact, part of a definite pattern which is governed by fixed, scientific laws, and a knowledge of these will help him to plan more accurately for the future and thus avoid the haphazard methods that so often characterize the work of the average fancier.

Most of the old-time writers on the subject were puzzled, for example, by the disappearance and reappearance in succeeding generations of cinnamon colored birds in some strains of canary, or by the fact that if two crested birds were mated together a proportion of the chicks died just before or just after hatching. This, of course, was in pre-Mendelian days, before the science of genetics had taught breeders to appreciate certain basic facts concerning a bird's hereditary constitution, and although a knowledge of this subject in its more advanced stages is not altogether necessary for the practical fancier, some of its simpler principles if properly understood can undoubtedly aid him in his work.

It may rightly be pointed out that none of the old-time fanciers had any knowledge of genetics and yet were often eminently successful in producing strains of birds of high quality, and possibly many of the leading breeders of today would also deny that they owed anything to the teachings of this science; but if their methods were closely examined it would probably be found either that from sheer practical experience they were using principles that have since been proved to be genetically sound, or that aided by a scientific background, similar results might well have been achieved in far less time and by less wasteful methods.

HEREDITY AND ENVIRONMENT

The first important essential for the fancier to appreciate is that every individual bird is the living embodiment of two distinct sets of factors, known respectively as 'heredity' and 'environment,' both of which are of equal importance to the final product. Thus a bird which, from an exhibition point of view, possesses an ideal hereditary constitution, if brought up in an unsatisfactory environment will never be able to develop its full potentialities; conversely, a bird that is genetically inferior can never be made into a winning show specimen even though given the benefit of perfect conditions.

Environment may be defined as the sum total of the conditions under which a bird lives that may have any possible bearing upon its development, and it includes most of the factors that have already been discussed in the chapters on Housing and Equipment, and Feeding and General Management and others that will be dealt with in the chapters on Molting and Exhibiting. All of these are, of course, wholly within the control of the individual fancier, hence the emphasis that has been laid upon care and attention to detail in these matters. But the really successful breeder is the one who, as far as is possible, is also able to bring the hereditary factors under his control, which is a much more difficult problem.

Just as environment may be regarded as the external influences upon the life of the bird, heredity may be defined as being the inborn forces that affect and guide its development —in other words those factors that it has inherited from its ancestors. The manner in which these factors are passed on from one generation to the next requires a little knowledge of biology and in particular, of the processes of reproduction.

THE MECHANISM OF HEREDITY

The body tissues of every living organism are composed of a number of minute units called *cells* which, in the higher forms of life, have mostly become specialized in their functions, such as those in feather, skin or nerve tissue, and the activity of each cell is controlled by its *nucleus* which may be regarded as a kind of 'brain center' embedded in the protoplasm of the cell. The nucleus contains a number of threadlike bodies called *chromosomes* which in their turn, rather like beads on a string, hold a number of still smaller particles of matter known as *genes*. Each of these genes may control the development of one or more distinct characteristics, and collectively they represent the entire hereditary make-up of the organism in question.

In order to be able to function at all, the chromosomes in all body cells have to be present in matched pairs and thus in every nucleus there is a double set of chromosomes, one set having been inherited from each parent; but when the sex cells are being formed by the reproductive tissue the pairs separate again, and only one set goes into each of the sex cells. Thus, when fertilization takes place and a male sperm unites with a female ovum, two complete sets of chromosomes are reassembled and the fertilized egg can start to develop. The sole physical link between the generations is through the sex cells, and it is at this stage that all of the inherited characteristics are passed on through the medium of the genes.

First of all the single fertilized egg cell splits into two, these two again divide and become four, four become eight and so on, as the developing embryo grows in complexity. At each cell division every chromosome splits evenly along its length, and a portion passes into each of the daughter cells so that every body cell becomes possessed of identical sets of chromosome pairs, all derived ultimately from the original fertilized egg cell which in its turn had received one set of chromosomes from each parent.

Upon this biological fact of inheriting from each parent one complete set of chromosomes which separate again when reproduction takes place, together with the genes that they carry, rests the whole conception of heredity.

MENDELISM

The first scientific inquiry into the inheritance of certain definite characteristics was carried out by Gregor Mendel (1822-1884), using plant material for his experiments. Unfortunately his work remained unknown to the world at large until the turn of the century; since when a vast amount of research has been done, both with plants and animals, in following up and developing the principles he discovered. Regrettably little work has been done however, in the case of canaries, owing to their being of no economic importance to man and to their relatively slow rate of reproduction.

Chart showing the inheritance of genes for tall and dwarf in garden peas.

Impure Tall (Td)
Sex Cells→T and d

	T		Result:
	TT	Td	25% Pure Tall (TT)
Impure Tall (Td)			50% Impure Tall (Td)
d	Td	dd	25% Pure Dwarf (dd)

In his first experiment Mendel turned his attention to a pair of contrasting characteristics found in garden peas, namely tallness and dwarfness of growth, and by means of hand pollination he crossed pure strains of the two types. The hybrids from this first cross (known as the first filial generation, or 'F1') when grown proved not to be intermediate in height as might have been expected but were all tall and, owing to the disappearance of the dwarfs in this cross, tall was described as being 'dominant' and dwarf as 'recessive' when the pair of genes representing these characteristics were brought together in the F1.

Next the F1 hybrids were self pollinated, and from their progeny (the second filial generation, or 'F2') it was found that approximately one quarter were dwarfs and the rest tall. Further tests showed that the dwarfs continued to breed true indefinitely when self pollinated, but among the talls only one third bred true while the others behaved in the manner of the F1 hybrids. It thus became clear that the two true breeding types were always producing sex cells pure for their particular characteristics, while the 'impure' tall peas of the F1 were producing sex cells of both types inherited from the original parents which during reproduction were able to re-combine.

It is customary to use a capital letter for the dominant characteristic, and its lower case counterpart for the recessive, thus tall should be represented by 'A' and dwarf by 'a', but in the interests of simplicity, the letters 'T' for 'tall' and 'd' for 'dwarf' have been used. Further experiments showed that when the impure tall peas were back-crossed with the pure dwarf ones, 50 per cent of each type were produced in their progeny as follows:

Chart showing the inheritance of genes for tall and dwarf in garden peas.

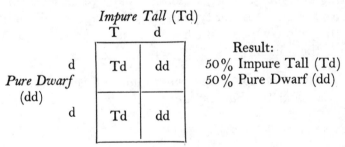

Similarly, when the impure tall peas were back-crossed with the pure tall ones, 50 per cent of each type were again produced, although in this instance as they were all tall the types were visually indistinguishable and could only be proved by their breeding performance. Many other experiments were carried out by Mendel in which other contrasting pairs of characteristics were involved, and in each case the results proved to be similar until eventually sufficient data was assembled to substantiate the Mendelian Theory of Inheritance. The name now given to true breeding types is 'homozygous,' and to impure breeding types 'heterozygous,' and the example described above, in which a cross between a heterozygous dominant and a homozygous recessive gives 50 per cent of each type among the progeny, is commonly found in the breeding of certain types of canary.

MENDELIAN INHERITANCE IN CANARIES

It must be appreciated by the beginner that the mathematical predictions of genetics are accurate only over a large sample. With a pair of canaries that may perhaps produce only eight youngsters in a season the 50-50 prediction may well not be manifest, but if it were possible for this pair to be kept breeding together until 100 young ones had been raised, the accuracy of the forecast would become evident. It is rather like the tossing of a coin in which a large number of throws would result in approximately half 'heads' and half 'tails,' whereas a small sample only could easily be all 'heads.'

1. *Yellow x Buff:* The most common example of Mendelian inheritance in canaries is to be found in the normally advised mating of yellow to buff, which gives an overall result of 50 per cent of each feather type in the offspring. In this mating it is the yellow which is the heterozygous dominant and buff that is the homozygous recessive:

Chart showing the inheritance of genes for yellow and buff in canaries.

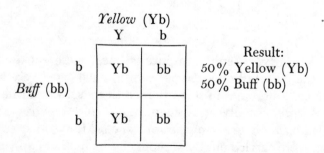

Result:
50% Yellow (Yb)
50% Buff (bb)

Owing to the widespread use of the yellow x buff mating by breeders most of the yellows are of the heterozygous type, but true breeding or homozygous yellows can be produced if desired by mating together two heterozygotes, following the same principle as self pollinating the F1 generation of garden peas in Mendel's experiments. The mating will produce 25 per cent homozygous yellows, 50 per cent heterozygous yellows and 25 per cent buffs and again, like the tall peas, the two types of yellow can only really be distinguished by their breeding results. Their outward appearance (*phenotype*) is alike, but their genetical make-up (*genotype*) is different. Breeders have never been in favor of these homozygous yellows as they generally have a tendency to be rather 'racy' birds with thin, brittle feathering, and the continued breeding together experimentally of homozygous yellows has produced birds in which the feather has been so deficient in substance as to be unable to cover the breast bone. The Italian 'Gibber Italicus' canary possesses this characteristic since all birds of the breed are homozygous yellows —there are no buffs.

If buffs are mated together in breeding they will continue to produce buff youngsters only, just as the dwarf peas bred true in Mendel's experiments. But this type of mating, known to breeders as 'double-buffing,' needs to be carefully supervised, otherwise it may eventually lead to the production of oversized, bulky, coarse-feathered birds.

2. *Crest x Plainhead:* This is another example of the heterozygous dominant x homozygous recessive mating, the dominant characteristic in question being the crest. Exhibition birds are bred by mating crest to plainhead, which gives the usual 50 per cent of each type among the offspring. A further point of interest here is that the homozygous crest cannot be produced by the mating together of two heterozygotes, owing to the fact that if the crested gene is present in both of the chromosome pairs it becomes lethal to the individual, which dies upon hatching or soon afterwards. It has been suggested that the crested characteristic is brought about by an abnormality in the structure of the skull which, although quite harmless in the single dose, becomes so great in double strength that the bones of the cranium do not properly close up.

79

Quite apart from the loss of the lethal chicks, this mating is not usually favored by fanciers as it is said to give rise to a number of birds that, from an exhibition point of view, are in some way unsatisfactory in the crest. It should also be noted than the plainheaded bird is pure for the plainhead characteristic and will breed true to that. Two plainheaded birds mated together cannot produce crests even though they themselves might have been bred from a crest x crest mating.

Chart showing the inheritance of genes for crest and plainhead in canaries.

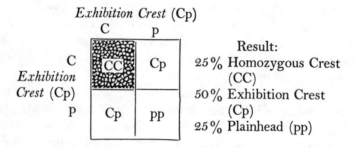

Exhibition Crest (Cp)

Result:
25% Homozygous Crest (CC)
50% Exhibition Crest (Cp)
25% Plainhead (pp)

3. *Dominant White Ground Color x Normal Ground Color:* Another example of a lethal effect being produced when a dominant characteristic is present in a double dose is to be found in the case of the dominant white canary. This particular mutation, coming from Germany just after the first World War, has now been introduced into most of the standard breeds. All dominant whites are heterozygotes, and normal yellow ground canaries are recessive to the dominant white characteristic so that the correct mating to apply is white x normal, which results in the usual 50 per cent of each color among the chicks. It is immaterial whether the normal bird of the pair is a yellow or a buff except that in the former case both yellow and buff may be produced among the normal chicks, whereas in the latter case they can only be buffs.

The mating of dominant white to dominant white is as wasteful as the crest x crest mating cited in the previous section, because 25 per cent of chicks that receive the double dose of the dominant white gene are non-viable.

4. *Variegation:* Not enough research has been done upon the subject of variegation and most authorities still quote the results of experiments carried out in Germany by Dr. Duncker, and published in 1929. From a total of 517 produced from 19 test matings he found that there was no case of dominance, as in the previous examples quoted, and if a dark self bird was mated to a clear the progeny were all intermediate in character, i.e. variegated. The variegated birds he regarded as being heterozygous for the manifestation of melanin pigment, and if inter-mated they produced 25 per cent self or foul, 50 per cent variegated and 25 per cent clear or ticked as follows:

Chart showing the inheritance of genes for self or foul and clear or ticked in birds.

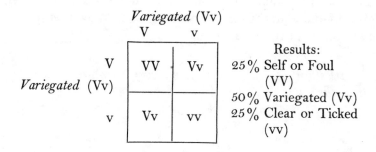

<table>
<tr><td colspan="3">Variegated (Vv)
V   v</td><td>Results:</td></tr>
</table>

Variegated (Vv)

	V	v
V	VV	Vv
v	Vv	vv

Results:
25% Self or Foul (VV)
50% Variegated (Vv)
25% Clear or Ticked (vv)

For practical application this supposition may be regarded as only broadly true for, as most fanciers will know, it is quite possible to find variegated youngsters among the progeny from a pair of clear birds. It must be remembered, however, that some clear birds possess a certain amount of dark underflue which is, of course, an expression of melanin pigment in the plumage although not shown on the actual web of the feather. Such birds therefore, which may be clear from a technical point of view, genetically may be variegated.

In most of the breeds of 'type' canaries the presence or absence of variegation is of little or no importance so that the fancier can usually select his breeding pairs relatively untroubled by the genetical aspects of this characteristic.

5. *Cinnamon Inheritance:* Self cinnamons form a small but not unimportant section of the Norwich canary fancy, and in other standard breeds also cinnamon marked, variegated or self birds are reasonably common, so that a knowledge of the workings of cinnamon inheritance can be useful to breeders of those varieties. The cinnamon mutation is one of the oldest in the canary world and was specifically mentioned by Hervieux in 1709. In view of similar incidences among wild birds it is possible that it occurred in wild caught, as well as in domesticated, canaries.

In the examples of Mendelism so far quoted the genetics have been quite simple and straightforward, but in the case of the melanin pigments they become rather more involved owing to the fact that the genes responsible happen to be located on the same chromosome that determines the sex of the individual, and thus we have what is known as a *sex-linked* mode of inheritance.

Chart showing the inheritance of sex chromosomes in birds.

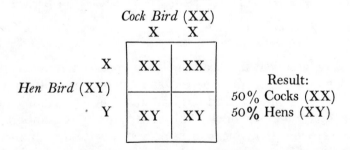

When dealing with the biological aspects of genetics it was pointed out that all body cells have two complete sets of chromosomes which become separated during the formation of the sex cells by the reproductive organs, but among these chromosome sets there is in fact one odd pair which are the ones responsible for sex determination. One is a complete chromosome, and is distinguished by the letter 'X', while the other is only rudimentary, and is denoted by the letter 'Y'. In his genetical make-up a cock bird possesses two X chromosomes, whereas a hen has an odd pair of one X and one Y, so that during breeding approximately 50 per cent of each sex are produced according to the familiar pattern.

Now, as the genes for the melanin pigments are located upon the X chromosome they are automatically linked with the determination of sex itself, and as cinnamon coloring is recessive to green the following facts will be apparent:

(a) A hen, because she possesses only the one X chromosome, must be either a pure breeding green or a pure breeding cinnamon, as there are no other alternatives.

(b) A cock however, can be of three distinct genotypes: (i) a pure breeding green with the green gene on each of his X chromosomes; (ii) a pure breeding cinnamon with the cinnamon gene on each of the X chromosomes, or (iii) a cinnamon 'carrier' with green on one chromosome and cinnamon on the other. In phenotype the bird is green, but it carries as a recessive the character for cinnamon which it can, of course, pass on during breeding, thus:

Chart showing the inheritance of genes for green and cinnamon in birds.

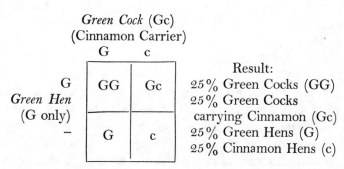

This was the mating that so often puzzled the old-time breeders who were mystified by the fact that from the mating of two greens a cinnamon could be produced.

The complete matings involving greens and cinnamons are given below, and when applying them it should be remembered that the distinguishing characteristic of the cinnamon is its *pink eye color*, whether the bird be a clear, ticked, variegated, foul or self. In the case of the green series the eye color is black. The actual production of colored pigment in the plumage depends upon the independent variegation factors which have already been discussed.

Parents	*Progeny*
1. Green cock, Green hen.	All Green.
2. Green cock, Cinnamon hen.	All Green but cocks are cinnamon carriers.
3. Cinnamon cock, Green hen.	Green cocks carrying cinnamon, Cinnamon hens.
4. Green cock carrying cinnamon, Green hen.	Green cocks, Green cocks carrying cinnamon, Green hens, Cinnamon Hens.
5. Green cock carrying·cinnamon, Cinnamon hen.	Green cocks carrying cinnamon, Cinnamon cocks, Green hens, Cinnamon hens.
6. Cinnamon cock, Cinnamon hen.	All Cinnamon.

There are several other recessive sex-linked characteristics in the canary, but as they are mainly of interest to color breeders or experimentalists they have not been included in this section.

VARIATION
In the foregoing paragraphs the breeder has been taught, according to the laws of genetics, what he may or may not expect from various matings commonly in use in canary breeding. What cannot be accurately foretold however, is something of far greater importance to most fanciers, namely the inheritance of particular show points by any individual.

The genotype of a bird will determine whether it will be a crest or a plainhead, a green or a cinnamon, a clear or a variegated, but whether or not it will be a *good* crest or a *good* cinnamon, from an exhibition point of view, is quite another matter. In a class of crested canaries, for example, all the birds are alike as far as the gene that gives rise to the crest is concerned, yet a close examination would reveal that the crests were not all identical and would enable a judge to place them in order of merit, according to how closely they approached the ideal as laid down by the specialist society.

The same is true of any group of birds of a particular breed, and such differences as exist between individuals are due to modifications brought about by several interacting factors both of an environmental and hereditary nature. It is upon such variable living material that the canary breeder must exercise his skill and endeavor to produce birds as near as he can get to perfection in his chosen variety.

SELECTION

The most obvious method that the breeder has at his command is that of the deliberate selection of his breeding pairs according to standards that have been laid down by the specialist societies. In this he differs from nature, where the only form of selection is that imposed by the harsh realities of the bird's environment, and it is quite certain that the cultivated breeds of canary would be unable to survive in the wild because most of their fancy points would prove to be a handicap.

That straightforward selection on a purely visual basis can prove effective is borne out by the certainty that most of our original 'type' breeds must have been produced in this way in the first place, but it is a relatively slow way of achieving results, since visual selection disregards the fact that a bird's appearance may be due as much to environmental factors as to hereditary ones.

Although several specified features are known to be of a dominant or recessive nature this is by no means an essential of all characteristics, many of which are intermediate, and this is especially true of most of the show points dealing with such things as bodily conformation, stance, wing carriage, feather quality, length of leg, and other such purely arbitrary qualities. There is, for example, no single gene for size of head, and if the breeder were to mate together two birds with large heads there is no certainty that all large-headed youngsters would appear among the progeny, although there would be a strong probability that some at least would possess this feature.

Following Mendelian principles however, if the first generation (the F1) were inter-mated, there is the likelihood that some form of segregation of genes would occur and individuals approaching the two parental types would be found among the F2. If the breeder were pursuing the point of large heads therefore, he would have to select the best of these to mate back to the grandparents in the reasonable expectation of producing a fair number of large-headed progeny.

BREEDING METHODS

Many skillful breeders have succeeded in building up strains of birds of such outstanding quality that they are immediately recognizable often by virtue of their superiority in certain distinctive points. This naturally cannot be achieved in a short time, but the fancier has recourse to certain well defined methods of approach to the problem, each of which is applied at one time or another by the majority of breeders.

1. *Inbreeding:* It may have taken a fancier many years to produce a few outstanding birds, and in order to retain their good points he will often mate them to closely related stock which he knows, or can assume, to be of similar hereditary constitution. Inbreeding always needs to be approached with caution, for besides establishing any good points that are possessed by parents it also brings to light any hidden bad points that might not at first have been apparent, and the fancier must be absolutely ruthless in culling these from his stock. In fact, he must be prepared in the first few generations of inbreeding to produce many more bad birds than good ones, and it needs a good deal of determination to continue when such disheartening results appear. In theory, inbreeding can continue indefinitely and several species of experimental

laboratory animals have been so bred for countless generations, once the initial 'weeding out' of unsatisfactory individuals has taken place; but fanciers in general rarely tend to go to such limits, especially when deterioration in stamina and declining fertility become increasingly apparent. There are several practical objections to the continued use of close inbreeding, especially for the fancier with a limited stock.

2. *Linebreeding:* This is a name given rather loosely to several differing systems of breeding procedure: (a) a rather less close form of inbreeding which involves mating cousin to cousin, uncle to niece, etc.; (b) continued breeding back to a particularly outstanding individual by mating him first to his daughters and then to the resulting granddaughters, etc.; (c) keeping several separate inbred lines going within a stud, so that when an outcross is needed it will be unnecessary to go outside for it. All of these systems are widely used in the canary fancy and are the chosen methods of some of the leading exponents of the art.

3. *Outbreeding:* By breeding from unrelated stock and introducing fresh blood every year or so, the fancier is using a system of outbreeding. This method generally produces increased stamina but a greater variability among the offspring, so that larger numbers need to be bred from which to select show specimens. Some authorities hold the view that this is as good a method as any to breed show livestock since, in any group of individuals of a particular breed, the natural variations that occur will provide a fair sample from which to choose the exhibition specimens.

4. *Advanced Methods:* Some of the modern techniques now applied to commercial livestock breeding, such as test-mating, progeny-testing or nucleus-breeding, have probably had no impact at all so far upon the hobby of canary breeding, although it is not improbable that in the future some of the more adventurous fanciers may adopt these principles.

PRACTICAL ISSUES

It is usually the ambition of the novice canary breeder eventually to produce a strain of birds of his own, which are true to a type and consistently successful in competition with other breeders of the same variety. But before progressing thus far, several practical points are bound to be considered.

1. *Initial Stock:* The acquisition of suitable foundation stock is the first problem, and although it may prove expensive a breeder will obviously be saved many years' work by starting with the very best birds obtainable. Preferably, these should come from one of the successful champion breeders most of whom have some surplus stock available each year, and will supply properly matched pairs if requested. If the cost is a limiting factor, and it is necessary to start with birds that are rather less perfect than hoped for, it would be a wise policy to purchase as soon as possible a really good cock bird that could be mated to home-bred hens in order to up-grade the stock.

2. *Maintaining a Standard:* It occasionally happens that the beginner, after a season or two of relative success, finds that instead of improving as hoped, his stock is actually deteriorating. This is almost certainly due to the fact that he was at first breeding with the carefully selected and properly matched pairs supplied to him by a champion breeder, and that when compelled to rely upon his own judgement in selecting his breeding pairs, he was lacking the necessary experience. At this stage he should not be too proud or embarrassed to seek the advice and guidance of the original breeder who, if he is a good fancier, will be only too willing to help him overcome his difficulties. To be a successful breeder it is a fundamental necessity to have a clear conception of what one is attempting to produce, and to exercise accurate judgement in arranging matings that will achieve this end.

3. *Improving Points:* When the fancier finds that he is at least maintaining the high standard of his initial stock, he may then feel that he is in a position actually to improve upon certain features of the breed. This he will have to do

on the principles of selection already described, by choosing individuals which clearly manifest the characteristic that he is hoping to accentuate, and following up with any necessary back-crossing in order to fix the point. It is almost always advisable to concentrate upon improving and establishing one point at a time, for in this way there is no side-tracking the issue by attempting to balance one point against another, and in so doing the fancier may well find that he has succeeded in perfecting some particular characteristic which will then be so apparent in his birds that he will, in effect, have produced a strain of his own.

ADDITIONAL READING

In a book embracing the whole field of the canary fancy any chapter dealing with the scientific aspects of breeding must necessarily be in some measure inadequate, and omission and over-simplification inevitable. For the reader who may wish to go more deeply into the matter there are several books on the general subject of livestock breeding, of which the classic is *Animal Breeding* by Dr. A.L. Hagedoorn (Holland). Dealing specifically with canaries, the most complete book is *New Coloured Canaries* by A.K. Gill (England), and in *Canary Matings in Polychrome* by E.H. Kerrison, Jr. (U.S.A.) all of the possible matings are set out in diagrammatic form, together with some theoretical ones that have not yet been bred. As both of these books were published in the early 1950's, neither is completely up to date in respect of some of the more recent mutations that have occurred in the realms of color breeding. This subject is well covered, however, by some more recent publications both in Holland and Germany among which may be mentiond *Het Grote Kanarienboek* by A. Rutgers.

7
Molting

Following hard upon the activities of the breeding season, for some fanciers the molt may prove to be something of an anticlimax—a kind of tiresome and tedious period that has to be endured before the final products of the breeding season can be properly appraised. On the other hand it can be one of the most interesting aspects of the hobby in which a remarkable transformation takes place, particularly where some breeds of canary are concerned, and it has often been said, with some degree of truth, that this is the time when champions are made or marred.

In their juvenile plumage many youngsters may have looked quite promising, but it is not until after the completion of their first molt that they can really be appreciated in their full maturity. Inevitably some disappointments may be in store, and some surprises too, since occasionally a bird thought little of before the molt commences can develop into an excellent show specimen by its close.

In effect this is the time when, rather than relax his efforts, the fancier should continue to give his fullest attention and provide his birds with the best possible conditions under which to develop their new plumage.

TIME FOR MOLTING

Generally speaking, the molting season as a whole extends from about the middle of July to the end of October, with perhaps a variation of a week or so either way according to local circumstances. No individual bird however, if in proper health, takes the entire three months over the process, which normally is of about 6 to 8 weeks' duration.

It should always be the endeavor of the fancier to secure a quick and successful molt, and to achieve this end it is essential to finish the breeding season in good time. Young birds hatched in July will not even commence to molt until September, which means that the later stages may well coincide with raw, damp days in November, and might even be prolonged into early December by which time the show season is half over. Furthermore, late and protracted molting often has far reaching effects in the following breeding season, when it will frequently be found that such retarded birds are unsatisfactory breeders in a number of ways.

An early molt during the still warm days of late summer and early autumn is the ideal situation at which to aim.

THE MOLTING PROCESS

Strange as it may seem, biologically speaking, feathers are modified scales, serving as a reminder perhaps that from an evolutionary point of view birds have descended from some remote, reptilian-type ancestor. The feathers develop from pits in the skin and grow in orderly lines only on certain areas of the body, which are known as feather tracts, but spread out to cover all parts when fully expanded.

There are two main types of feather to be recognized: 1. The contour, or 'body feathers,' with which the body itself is clothed and protected, and 2. The quill, or 'flight feathers,' which are concerned with the process of flying and consist of the tail feathers, and the primary and secondary flights of the wings. Young birds of the current year do not shed these at their first molt but retain them until the following year, and it is during this period that they are known as 'unflighted' birds.

The new feathers develop from the same pits from which the old ones are shed, the process being somewhat analogous to the replacement of milk teeth in mammals by the permanent set, and the growing feather follicle draws its nourishment from the bloodstream through a small opening at the base of the feather. Molting does not occur in any haphazard fashion but follows a definite ordered pattern, commencing with the feathers on the wing butts and pectoral tracts, and from thence extending gradually over the whole body finishing up on the head and neck. Thus a bird just beginning to molt will show fresh color in two small lines on each side of the breast and at the shoulder, whereas one in which the molt is almost complete will probably still have just a few 'pin' feathers (i.e. feathers not fully burst from their sheaths) around the face and eyes.

CAGING

There is little doubt that the quickest and most satisfactory molting could be achieved in aviaries under natural conditions, but since this is clearly not practicable with exhibition stock, owing to the near certainty of the new plumage becoming quickly soiled, it is invariably the practice for all birds to be molted in cages.

In the past, fanciers frequently took extraordinary trouble over the molting of their birds and many breeders made use of specially constructed cages for the purpose. These were generally somewhat smaller than the usual single compartment breeding cage, and often had provision for a sheet of glass or a wooden shutter to be attached to the front in order to exclude drafts and dust, or to subdue the light. Some were even said to line their molting cages with flannel to minimize the possibility of damage to the new feathers.

Although there is nothing against the fancier making use of special devices of this kind should he so wish, these practices have now largely fallen into disuse and it is admitted that during the molt, no less than any other time, the usual rules of hygiene should apply—namely, plenty of fresh air and exercise without drafts, damp, or fluctuating temperatures.

As is suggested in the chapter on Housing and Equipment, the double-compartment breeding cage provides very suitable accommodation during the molt for from two to six birds according to the nature of the occupants. Before molting commences the birds will, in all probability, have already been separated off, either singly or in couples, into each compartment, which is about the best arrangement for caging them during this period. If accommodation is restricted however, it is quite permissable to molt them in small groups of about five or six in the full double cage, although this method has certain dangers attached to it. Should there happen to be a mischievous 'plucker' among them there is the obvious risk of having a greater number of birds spoiled for show.

The most satisfactory arrangement if lack of space is the limiting factor, is to give the best of the cage accommodation to the most promising birds and then group up the remainder, including much of the older breeding stock and any others that may be past their prime as exhibition material.

GENERAL MANAGEMENT

Although the production of a new set of feathers must of necessity impose some strain upon the system, it should not be forgotten that the process is a perfectly natural one and that the birds are in no sense unwell as was at one time supposed. They are usually rather less active at this period but do not need to be coddled or treated as semi-invalids in any way.

Special draft-proof cages have already been mentioned as one of the precautions taken by fanciers in former days, and yet another was the system of molting the birds in semi-darkness by hanging heavy curtains over the cages or even, as was sometimes practiced, pasting brown paper over the entire cage front, leaving only the seed box and drinker holes uncovered. The idea behind this, quite apart from that of keeping the birds steady and quiet, was to prevent any possibility of the color of the new feathers fading by exposure to light, but to what extent ultra-violet rays affect the color pigments in the feathers of birds has probably never been determined. A wise precaution however would be to prevent any *direct* sunlight from falling upon the molting cages, and this could quite easily be achieved by having the birdroom windows fitted with light curtains which could be drawn across whenever necessary.

Regular use of the bath must be considered as important not only because the vigorous splashing involved helps to loosen the old feathers, but because the subsequent preening is beneficial to the new plumage. Many fanciers advocate daily bathing during the molting period, but if this frequency cannot be conveniently arranged it should certainly not be less than once a week. Baths should not be offered late in the day however, owing to the possibility of the birds going to roost with the plumage still wet. In the event of any bird refusing to bathe, an occasional light spraying with a hand syringe whenever time permits will prove helpful to the new plumage.

Some fanciers are inclined to avoid many of the routine cleaning jobs during the molting season, being under the impression that any disturbances may cause the birds to 'stick in the molt'. It is true that a *severe* shock, or indeed a chill or any temporary loss of health, may cause this undesirable check to the molting process, but in a well organized birdroom the event is unlikely and in any case, in the interests of hygiene, the health of the stock as a whole is more important than the possibility of odd individuals becoming checked in the molt.

Now and again birds may be encountered which have developed the vice of feather plucking, that is pulling feathers out of their companions' plumage, usually from the region of the back and rump. This is almost always aggravated, if not actually caused, by overcrowding, so that avoidance of the trouble at the outset is in the hands of the fancier. If it should occur, some distraction for the birds can be provided in the form of partly unravelled string tied to the cage fronts for them to peck at, but it is always preferable to detect the culprit, who should then be removed and caged alone.

FEEDING

Feeding during the molt needs to be on the generous side for not only has the normal bodily metabolism to be maintained, but additional material must be supplied for the development of the new feathers and, in the case of current year birds, for actual body growth, which still continues to some extent. Generous feeding however, must never be allowed to develop into overfeeding since the birds are rather less active physically at this period and the lack of exercise may lead to their becoming overfat, with perhaps a disposition towards liver complaints.

Feather tissue is almost entirely formed from protein so that it is mainly with this substance that the feeding must be supplemented. The staple seed mixture can be enriched by the addition of high protein seeds but, as these tend also to be high in oil content, in most cases the extra nourishment will be supplied in the form of egg food or one of its substitutes. With the exception of varieties that are being color-fed, and who will therefore receive a small helping daily in any case, a little egg food can be given to most breeds of canary two or three times weekly so long as molting continues.

It should be noted that at this time of the year ripe wild seeds are generally plentiful and are very beneficial to health, quite apart from the obvious pleasure that the birds derive from working over the bunches of seed heads that are provided. Chickweed, shepherd's purse, thistle, plantain, dock, sowthistle, lettuce, seeding grasses and many others will be accepted with relish, with the usual proviso that they have been gathered from uncontaminated sources.

Greenfood also is a valuable daily addition to the diet, not only for its vitamin and mineral content but because it contains a chemical substance called *xanthophyll*, or *lutein*, which is essential for the formation of the yellow pigment in the feathers of canaries. Birds which are molted on an abundant supply of dark green leaves, such as those of kale or spinach, show a marked improvement in the richness of their yellow coloring—a fact well appreciated by the breeders of non-color-fed varieties.

COLOR FEEDING

It will be obvious that in its wider sense all canaries are color fed, since it is solely from the food that they eat during the molt that color pigments are derived. Experiments carried out in Germany in 1934 proved that when fed on a completely lutein-free diet, yellow canaries molted out white, as there was nothing in their food from which the body processes could manufacture the necessary yellow pigments.

To the canary fancy in general however, the term 'color feeding' has a special significance and refers to a special type of feeding administered to certain breeds of canary, which is designed to turn the basic yellow ground color to orange. The practice has an interesting historical background.

History: In the middle of the nineteenth century the leading show variety of canary whose popularity exceeded that of all others combined was the Norwich—a very different bird in those days from the modern type. At that period its main attribute was its color for which 45 points out of 100 were allowed, so that it is small wonder that a good deal of attention was given to this particular feature. In order to improve the bird's natural color during the molt many extraordinary concoctions, as well as natural preparations, were employed, some of which were undoubtedly useful for the purpose intended and others quite valueless. Among them were such items as marigold flowers, saffron cake, egg yolk, beetroot and carrot with saffron or cochineal solutions in the drinkers. Artificial coloring externally by means of vegetables dyes was also frequently practiced by some unscrupulous exhibitors, presenting the judges of the day with the added responsibility of detecting and disqualifying such exhibits.

The whole story of the origin of color feeding as we know it is given in *The Book of Canaries and Cage Birds*, by the great Victorian authority W.A. Blakston who was intimately connected with the affair. It appears that in the early 1870's some birds were being exhibited which astonished the whole fancy in that their color was quite definitely orange, as opposed to the deep golden-yellow which was the best that had previously been produced. Not unnaturally they were regarded with suspicion, and on two separate occasions protests led to their being subjected to examination by the public analyst, who in each case was obliged to certify that there was no evidence of artificial coloring matter upon the plumage.

Although some of the more unscrupulous owners tried to maintain that the superior color of their birds was due to selective breeding, word gradually got around that it was in fact due to special feeding, and the details were eventually made public in the *Journal of Horticulture* of December 11th, 1873, by E. Bemrose of Derby, who revealed that the orange coloring of the plumage was induced by feeding the

RED FACTOR CANARY. A bronze ino rose pastel cock. One of the newest mutations, this bird is, in fact, a "self" although the melanins show only as faint brown markings.

birds cayenne pepper while they were molting.

A rather chaotic period followed in which classes were provided at the shows for 'K-N fed,' 'Non K-N fed' and 'Natural Color' birds, but the dividing line between them was often so tenuous that a bird was able to compete in one section one week and in another the next, or alternatively, to win under one judge and be disqualified by another! In due course it became accepted that the only trustworthy exhibits were the openly admitted color-fed ones, and this eventually became the standard practice.

Some objections were raised at first to the custom of cayenne feeding on the grounds that such a pungent substance must be injurious to the digestive system, but quite apart from the fact that the birds ate it readily, it was subsequently discovered that the 'hot' ingredient of the pepper had nothing at all to do with the color produced, and that equally good results were to be obtained from tasteless red peppers.

Color Feeding Practice: Color feeding today has developed beyond those early stages and many fanciers' suppliers provide under various trade names ready prepared color foods, of which the basic ingredient is the finely ground pods of the salad plant *Capsicum annum grossum*—a sweet or tasteless 'pepper'.

The intention, as has already been explained, is to convert a basically yellow bird into an orange one, but as this change is not of a permanent nature it has to be repeated at each successive molt otherwise the bird will revert to its normal yellow plumage. Not all breeds of canary are so treated, and the beginner is sometimes influenced in his initial choice of variety by whether or not he will be obliged to carry out this practice. However, since the amount of trouble involved is very little indeed over and above that of normal molting feeding, no objection to a color-fed breed need be made on that score alone. In fact, apart from Red Factor canaries which are fed food preparations containing canthaxanthin, only the Norwich, the Lizard and the Yorkshire are color-fed.

The aim is always to produce as deep and rich a color as possible, but it must be appreciated that a good *natural* color must first be bred for, and is a necessary prerequisite to successful color feeding. A bird that is naturally pale will never come through really deep in tone, no matter how well fed.

As with breeding systems so it is with color feeding, and fanciers often tend to have their own favorite ideas on the subject. Many methods can be employed but it is probably true to say that the majority of present-day breeders use one of the proprietary brands of color food, mixing it in accordance with the makers' directions, and this is usually the simplest and most satisfactory method for the beginner to adopt.

The most widely used medium for administering color food to canaries is the ordinary soft food mixture, made with or without egg as may be thought necessary, into which a quantity of the basic color food has been incorporated. It is usual to begin this feeding well before the molt commences with a fairly weak mixture of about 1 part of color food to 10 or 12 parts of soft food, gradually increasing the strength week by week until it is in the proportion of about 1 part of color food to 3 or 4 parts of soft food by the time the birds are starting to drop their first feathers.

The chief secret of success lies not, as might be thought, in cramming as much rich color food as possible into the birds, but in giving it regularly and in moderate strength. A small teaspoonful per bird daily is generally eaten with relish, whereas large quantities given in too concentrated a form may merely succeed in turning them against it. A further point of importance is to continue with the feeding for some time after the molt has apparently finished, as there may be feathers still coming through that are not immediately visible to the eye. Many exhibitors also give a little color food once or twice a week throughout the show season, as a precaution against any feathers that may be accidentally shed being replaced by the natural yellow color.

Occasionally birds are to be found that do not take very readily to eating color food, but they can generally be induced to do so either by incorporating a little honey or syrup with the mixture or by adding some of their favorite soaked

YORKSHIRE CANARY. A cinnamon variegated buff showing all sorts of faults in this particular photograph.

RED FACTOR CANARY. A frosted rose pastel (or rose ivory) hen. The delicate rose pink of this mutation does not show up well in this photograph.

seeds. Indeed some fanciers continue to supply soaked seed in any case during the molt, and it is often a matter of convenience to mix it in bulk (after washing) into the color food so that the two can be given in one vessel.

Color feeding preparations containing canthaxanthin are now freely used in the molting of Norwich, Lizard and Yorkshire canaries as well as for the Red Factors which it was originally employed.

CONCLUSION OF THE MOLT

At the end of the molt it still needs a week or so for the birds to be really 'hardened off,' and during this period the plumage, which has hitherto been somewhat soft and loose, becomes more compact and tightly braced giving the appearance so desired in most breeds of canary. It is now the aim of the fancier to tone up the bird's system after the strain imposed by molting so that it will be in fit condition for the shows that are soon to follow.

The majority of birds possessing a naturally robust constitution will probably need no special treatment and will come into hard condition as a matter of course, but there may be others that for one reason or another will need more liberal treatment in order to achieve that end. Some fanciers believe in the use of chemical tonics at this stage, and it was often advised in the older manuals that a few grains of citrate of iron or sulphate of iron should be added to the drinking water two or three times a week.

It is particularly important to keep the new plumage in perfect condition as long as possible, so that scrupulous cleanliness in the birdroom continues to be essential. If this rule is strictly adhered to it frequently avoids the necessity of having to handwash the show birds at some time during the exhibition season.

8

Exhibiting

Although the breeding season might be regarded by many as the center of the year's activities, it is really only the means to an end, the ultimate object for most breeders being to enter into friendly rivalry with their fellow fanciers at the shows.

This is done in most instances not with any special view to capturing all the trophies and monetary awards, which in any case are usually quite small, but with the object of ensuring that their breeding efforts are giving the desired results by producing birds equal to, if not better than, those of others. It is only by actually comparing birds side by side on the showbench that an accurate assessment of them can be made, and all too often it has been the lot of the uncritical fancier to find that his self-styled winners have turned out to be nothing more than also-rans when impartially judged. Conversely, many a fancier keeping birds in only a modest way has been pleasantly surprised when he has been persuaded to try his luck on the show-bench.

Apart from this aspect however, bird shows provide the ideal social occasion when fanciers are able to meet together to discuss points, compare notes and exchange information, and it is perhaps here more than anywhere else that by keeping his eyes and ears open the newcomer can learn something of the 'secrets' of the canary fancy.

The shows must also be regarded as the main shop window of the fancy, for they usually provide the only occasion on which members of the public see anything of the hobby and not infrequently they become useful recruiting centers for new members. For this reason alone all breeders of canaries should endeavor to give their support whenever circum-

RED FACTOR CANARY. The very pale dilution of the melanin pigments can be seen in the wings and on the back of this frosted bronze opal cock.

RED FACTOR CANARY. The delightful rose ground color and the faint brown markings are the characteristics of this bronze ino rose pastel cock bird.

stances permit, and this applies equally to the small-scale hobbyist, who may be limited to two or three shows only, and to the fancier whose larger resources may allow him to have a team of birds competing somewhere or other practically every week.

TYPES OF EXHIBITION

A large number of cage bird shows are held annually ranging in size from small local events to large international exhibitions, and the beginner will need to know something of what to expect in the way of competition at the various recognized types of show.

1. *Local Societies Members' Shows:* Participation in these is restricted to members of the society only and no 'outside' entry is accepted, although in many cases there is a purely nominal qualifying period for new members before becoming eligible. Where membership is small the annual show may attract an entry of only a hundred or so exhibits, but in the case of large, flourishing societies in well-populated areas this may well be nearer a thousand. Quite apart from their main annual show, the local societies often hold 'pairs' shows and 'young stock' shows for the benefit of their members—usually in February and July, respectively.

2. *Open Shows:* These shows are promoted and organized by the local societies either in addition to, or instead of their own members' annual fixture. They provide the most searching type of competition for the serious exhibitor since, owing to the fact that entry is completely unrestricted and may come from anywhere in the country, he will be taking on all comers and not merely the fellow members of his own local club.

3. *Specialist Societies' Shows:* Usually only the really big specialist societies are in a position to be able to stage their own shows. The majority give their 'patronage' to selected open events, and their members agree to send to these particular shows for the mutual benefit of both the specialist society and the show promoters.

SHOW CAGES AND CASES

In most branches of livestock keeping the show authorities provide special exhibition pens for the competitors, but owing to the obvious difficulties and risks involved in the handling of small birds that is not usually the case in the cage bird fancy. Every exhibitor therefore is required to send his birds to the show all ready in the cages which they will occupy throughout its duration.

Approved British show cage design: Norwich.

RED FACTOR CANARY. Apricot hen. This is the "buff" counterpart in Red Factors, sometimes referred to as "frosted" or "non-intensive."

PAIR OF NORWICH CANARIES. A clear buff cock and a variegated yellow hen well matched for breeding.

Approved British show cage design: Yorkshire.

Facing page:
Approved British show cage designs: Border Fancy (top), Gloster Fancy (bottom).

GLOSTER FANCY CANARY. A good type of consort with a broad, well rounded head and full eyebrow.

RED FACTOR CANARY. A frosted opal bronze cock. The melanin
pigments are very much diluted in this mutation.

At one time in the past there was no uniformity in these cages, each fancier using a design that he thought showed his own birds to advantage; but standard show cages have been approved by the various specialist societies as being most suitable for each particular breed, and these are the only ones acceptable today. Not only has this resulted in a general improvement in the presentation of the exhibits on the benches, but in absolute fairness to all competitors. Standard show cages are obtainable from most suppliers but it is quite permissible for the fancier to make his own, always provided that he complies accurately with the specifications laid down. The relevant details of these will be given in the appropriate chapters on each breed.

As most of the journeys to and from the shows will in all probability be by car, rail or air, it will be necessary to have strong but light traveling cases into which the show cages can be placed. These are usually constructed of plywood or hardboard, and will invariably need reinforcement at each corner, efficient snap fasteners and a strong carrying handle. The beginner will naturally have to decide on his own requirements in the matter but, as a start, it is suggested that carrying cases for two, three and four cages be provided, which in various combinations will enable him to send out any number of birds between two and nine.

TRAINING

Some show-training is necessary in order to teach a bird to display itself to advantage in front of the judge, since an otherwise excellent specimen that has been inadequately trained can be a source of great disappointment to its owner. The very least that is required of it is that it should stand quite still when being examined and not flutter about the cage, for although judges will do all that they can to give a fair viewing to all exhibits, they naturally cannot allow themselves unlimited time on an unsteady bird.

As was stated in Chapter 5, soon after the young canaries have been weaned they can be encouraged to become familiar with a show cage by hanging one on the front of their stock cage, both doors being open to allow them free

Early show cage training. Young Border Fancies in a show cage that has been hung on the front of their stock cage.

access from one to the other. Since it is always advisable to avoid handling the birds any more than is necessary it is essential to teach them to enter the cage on command, and this can be attempted as soon as they have gained confidence, by guiding them gently in with a long, thin cane known as a training stick.

Once the birds are used to doing this, the next stage is to remove the show cage with a bird inside it by carefully slipping the hand between the two open doors which are then safely closed. On finding itself inside thus isolated from its companions the young bird may perhaps show some panic and flutter about for a short while, but if the cage is placed on the birdroom table and the bird spoken to reassuringly it will soon settle down. According to the number of cages available several young birds can be dealt with at each training session, and if they are placed in view of one another as they would be on the show bench, they will soon become accustomed to the procedure.

RED FACTOR CANARY. A melanin pastel apricot (frosted red) cock.

NEW COLOR CANARY. An opal recessive fawn. This is the opal mutation in a fawn canary of the recessive white series.

The next phase of the training requires a fair degree of patience, for it is now necessary to encourage each bird to adopt the ideal position representative of its breed, and this is of particular importance with varieties such as the Yorkshire and the Border Fancy, where position and carriage of the body are allocated a definite value in the scale of points. In spite of the fact that the carrying handle is placed there, never handle the cage from the top for this will almost always cause a bird to crouch, which is a serious fault in all varieties. By touching the wires gently with the training stick, scratching the bottom of the cage with the fingernail, using the hand to engage the bird's attention, and by any similar means every effort should be made to pose the bird in the desired attitude and make it remain there for a few seconds.

Too much must not be expected of the birds at first, but after a few lessons they will soon know what is required of them and will respond accordingly. Some fanciers take their birds into the house so that they may become used to strange noises and movement, and this will also enable them to become accustomed to artificial lighting. As the training progresses they may be left in their show cages for increasingly longer periods, bearing in mind the fact that at most open shows they will be there for two days plus traveling time.

It will be appreciated that all potential show birds will need this sort of treatment, so that the fancier must be prepared to spend a fair amount of time on them during their training period, but the advantages of a well-trained bird as against an unsteady one makes the effort well worth while.

ENTERING

When wishing to enter his birds for a show the fancier must first obtain a *Schedule* of the classes provided. In the case of local shows these are usually dispatched automatically to all members of the club concerned, but with open shows they must be sent for. During the show season all the open events are widely advertised in the fancy's press, and all that is necessary is to write to the secretary, whose address will be in the advertisement, asking for a schedule to be forwarded.

In the canary fancy there are two recognized categories of exhibitor, the *Novice* and the *Champion*. There may be some variation in the rule as adopted by different clubs, but a widely accepted definition of a novice exhibitor is any person who at the time of entry has never won a first prize in Champion classes, or three first prizes in Novice classes, at any open show. Prizes won in classes with less than three exhibitors and ten staged exhibits do not count, neither do wins in Selling classes or in any other event where competition is not fully open. Generally speaking, anyone commencing the season as a Novice is entitled to retain that status throughout the season, irrespective of the number of wins he may gain.

Examination of the schedule will reveal that separate classes are provided for champion and novice exhibitors, and thus the beginner should make no mistake in his entries, which should be placed on the special entry form that is enclosed with the schedule. Reference to Chapter 10 will en-

Handwashing. Meticulous exhibitors will often handwash a bird a few days before an important show.

YORKSHIRE CANARY. A clear yellow hen. Yellow hens often show a little "frosting" around the neck.

BORDER FANCY CANARY. This yellow has a faint grizzled variegation mark on the back of its neck small enough in size to be classified as a "ticked" bird.

able him to verify such terms as yellow and buff, flighted and unflighted, clear, ticked or variegated, and so on, but if he has any difficulty in making his entries the help of an experienced fancier should be sought. This must be done in good time, for in the interests of efficient organization, most of the shows have a closing date for entries to be received, after which none will be accepted.

PREPARATION

Quite apart from the continued training of any individuals that may be necessary according to their responsiveness, or lack of it, the fancier will find himself obliged to make other preparations before his entries are fit to send out to the shows.

It has already been emphasized that after the completion of the molt it is desirable to keep the new plumage clean and in good condition, so as to avoid if possible the task of hand-washing the birds; but if they do happen to become dirty, as is so often the case in industrial areas, hand-washing may have to be undertaken. Like so many other simple, practical tasks, a demonstration is usually far more effective than pages of description in a book, and for this reason most of the cage bird societies arrange for at least one hand-washing demonstration each year, given by one of their 'old hands' for the benefit of the beginner. If at all possible, the newcomer should make a point of attending such a demonstration or, failing this, he may be able to persuade an experienced fancier friend to assist him in the matter.

If it does become necessary, any hand-washing should be done several days before the show to allow the plumage to tighten up again and to regain its 'bloom'.

A few days before the show the cage and traveling case labels will be received from the secretary, and these must be fixed in accordance with instructions, and the cages prepared for exhibition in the approved way. The wise fancier will already have overhauled them so that they are smart and clean, but if not, this must not be left until the last minute for if any touching up with the paint brush is found to be necessary they may not be completely dry in time for the show.

122

The floor covering of show cages differs from breed to breed, each specialist society laying down what it considers to be best for its own variety. Some simply have a good layer of plain canary seed which serves both as a floor covering and a seed supply, others use oat husks and still others, plain white blotting paper. If no standard is laid down it is recommended that thick white blotting paper be used as a base on account of its absorbent qualities, irrespective of whether seed is also added, but sand or sawdust should never be used in show cages. An adequate supply of seed must be placed in the cage to last for the duration of the show.

DISPATCH

Apart from those fortunate fanciers who are able to take their birds to the show by road, the majority have to send them by air or, in many European countries, by rail. Show catalogues will provide details on how to address them, and it will be important to verify plane and train schedules so that the birds will be met both going and returning. It is better to allow a safety margin, for having gone to so much trouble, it is a source of annoyance to have one's exhibits marked 'Arrived too late for judging'. Often a club will arrange a clearing house for a member to take others' birds along when taking his own to another show.

Everything now being ready it is only necessary to run the birds into the cages that have been prepared for them, and to allow them a short time to settle down before packing them into the traveling cases. A careful check should be made at this stage to ensure that each bird has been placed in its correct cage, that is, the one with the appropriate class label on it, for once dispatched, errors cannot be rectified and a judge coming across, say, a yellow bird in a class of buffs has no alternative but to mark it 'Wrong class'.

When placing the cages inside the case it is a wise plan to have a piece of cardboard or similar material to slip between them, in order to prevent any bird from getting its tail caught and possibly damaged between the wires. It is also worth while trying to envisage the rough handling, jarring and vibration that the cases are likely to encounter while on their journey, and to attempt to minimize their effect by

BORDER FANCY CANARIES. A matched pair consisting of an eye and wing marked bird on the left and a self green on the right.

RED FACTOR CANARY. The lipochrome pastel mutation is recessive and sex-linked so that rose pastels can easily be bred with normal red factors if records of their inheritance are carefully kept.

placing a layer of foam plastic on the floor of the case, to absorb the shock to some extent. It is also useful to fold wedges of newspaper to push into each corner to prevent the cages from rattling about.

One final point is not to forget to send the show cage drinkers, which should be separately wrapped and place inside the case.

Unless he is able to visit the show, which incidentally he should make every effort to do for his own edification, the fancier will not see his birds again until they are returned a few days later. To avoid any delay, arrangements should be made to collect them from the station to ensure that someone is at home to receive and unpack them and attend to their wants. It may be that after their experiences at the show the birds appear a little jaded, but after a drink and a tidbit of some favorite seed they soon revive, and if not too late in the day, a bath will usually be appreciated and will aid their quick recovery.

Because of the strain imposed upon the constitution of even the more robust bird, it is inadvisable to show any individual too often—perhaps three or four times in the season, with a wide interval between, being the limit that a beginner should expect. A bird that has been overshown sometimes takes a long time to recover, and frequently proves disappointing in the following breeding season.

AT THE SHOW

For the benefit of those who are unable to visit the shows, and others who may be unaware of what goes on behind the scenes, the following is a brief account of what happens.

On the day previous to the show a willing band of helpers from the promoting society will have been busy preparing the hall and erecting the staging ready for the cages, under the direction of the Show Manager. By the early evening, some early exhibits may already be arriving and these will be carefully checked against the Show Secretary's Entry Book, and then taken to their appropriate places on the benches where they are watered and then left to settle down.

Officials are on duty throughout the night to safeguard the exhibits, and by early morning on the day of the show the hall again becomes a very busy place. The remainder of the exhibits will be arriving and when these are all in, a thorough check is then made, class by class, to ensure that all exhibits have arrived and have had their wants properly attended to, so that everything is ready for judging to commence.

It is generally the aim to have this completed by lunch time, so that the show can be opened to the public by early afternoon.

Stewarding: Every cage bird society in the country is fortunate in having among its members a number of keen and active workers who give of their services unhesitatingly at the time of the shows. These are the people who, having labored at preparing the show hall on the previous day, invariably continue to act as stewards during the show itself. They fetch and carry the cages to and from the judges' bench, re-arrange them in their correct order after the awards have been made, stick the award labels on the appropriate cages and generally keep an eye on things when the public is admitted. There is no surer way for the newcomer to learn the routine working of a cage bird show than to volunteer his services as a steward.

Judging: Except in the case of the Roller canary, which is awarded points for its song passages, the judging of canaries takes place on the basis of visual comparison. One class at a time is placed before the judge, who then arranges the birds in order of merit according to the standards laid down by the specialist societies. Awards placed are: First, Second, Third, Fourth, Very Highly Commended, Highly Commended and Commended, but usually only the first three have any monetary value. Apart from the class winners however, there are special prizes to be competed for, such as: 'Best Hen,' 'Best Adult,' 'Best Novice,' 'Best Champion,' 'Best of Breed,' and so on, and it is when his birds first figure among the 'specials' that the fancier really begins to feel that he is 'getting somewhere.'

127

RED FACTOR CANARY. This red orange cock is the result of many years of work following the introduction of red genes into the canary by crossing with the Black-hooded Red Siskin (*Spinus cuculatus*).

9

Diseases and Parasites

In any handbook dealing with the general aspects of livestock keeping, it is customary to include a chapter on diseases and parasites, the tendency sometimes being to cover the subject so thoroughly that the reader may well become apprehensive at the multiplicity of ailments to which his pets are susceptible. The fact is, however, that under conditions of efficient management canaries rarely give any cause for alarm, the incidence of sick birds being negligible and deaths, except from old age, a rarity. Indeed, if it is made a regular practice to dispose of surplus birds before they reach the age of, say, three or four years, mortality among adult stock can practically be eliminated.

In spite of this, no fancier can afford to ignore altogether the subject of disease, although if he is sensible his efforts will be directed towards its prevention rather than its cure. With this in view, his priorities should be (a) the avoidance of disease by adopting sound methods of management, (b) the recognition of diseases if they do occur, and (c) the application of correct remedies for their treatment and control.

PREVENTIVE MEASURES

The most positive approach that a fancier can make is to embrace the sound breeding principles advised in Chapter 5, and refuse to breed with anything other than perfectly healthy stock. It may be true to say that few, if any, avian diseases are directly hereditable, but studies have shown that resistance or susceptibility to disease definitely are, and thus if any lack of vigor becomes inherent in the stock the birds will always be predisposed to any infection that may be go-

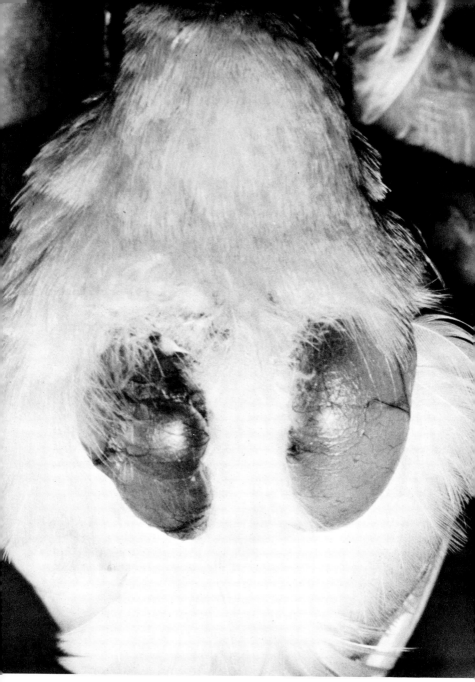

A canary with herniated clavicular air sacs. The affliction becomes very evident when the head of the bird is held down. Photo by L. Arnall. (From *BIRD DISEASES* by Drs. L. Arnall and I.F. Keymer, T.F.H. Publications, Inc.)

ing. There is always a temptation to overlook any slight defect in the health of an otherwise excellent show specimen, in the hope of breeding a few sound youngsters, but such a course can only lead to eventual disappointment, not necessarily in the first generation, but probably later on, especially where inbreeding is practiced.

The nature and importance of various food substances in the diet have already been dealt with, and reference has been made to the balance that is necessary between proteins, carbohydrates and fats and the essential minerals and vitamins, so that the fancier will readily appreciate the fact that correct feeding is another step he can take in promoting positive health among his stock. It is not sufficient merely to see that the food provided is of a suitable type and quality, but care must always be exercised in ensuring that it is perfectly fresh and free from any sort of contamination. Although this is particularly applicable to such items as greenstuff and wild seeds other sources must not be overlooked, and any temptation on the grounds of economy to use up old stocks of seed and other foods, which might possibly have become stale must be firmly rejected, since the saving of a few pennies may well prove to be expensive in the long run. Another fruitful source of trouble lies in allowing stale food to remain within the cages, and it should always be made a regular practice to remove, not later than the following day any unconsumed food, greenstuff or soaked seed, which can deteriorate rapidly especially during the summer months.

The necessity for clean, airy, draft- and damp-proof quarters has been sufficiently emphasized in an earlier chapter, as were the details of the routine cleansing recommended both for the cages and the birdroom itself. Even when these are strictly adhered to however, situations may still arise, usually through thoughtlessness, which could nullify all the previous care taken, and it is always advisable to be on the alert for any possible sources of infection and to make it a principle to be a little fussy over matters of hygiene.

Probably one of the commonest errors is the introduction of new birds into the stock without first ensuring their physical fitness, for however impeccable their origins, it is always wise to subject them to a period of quarantine until it can be safely assumed that they carry neither diseases nor parasites. If room cannot be found for them in the house for a few days, it should be possible to arrange for a special isolation cage within the birdroom, which would preclude any possibility of contact with other cages or their inmates. So little is definitely known about the diseases of birds that any period of quarantine can only be carried out on a basis of pure guesswork, but possibly ten days to a fortnight would be a fair assessment, after which, if no trouble is suspected, the new birds could be introduced with reasonable safety.

Another sensible precaution to take, which nevertheless is often overlooked either through lack of thought or laziness, is never to transfer a bird to a dirty cage. It should always be made a rule to clean and disinfect any cage that has recently been vacated, so that it will be ready for a new occupant at any time.

The shows provide yet another possible source of infection, more perhaps, of parasites than of disease, for not all fanciers are quite so particular about hygiene as they might be. Therefore when birds are returned from the shows a close watch should be kept on them for several days, and no time should be lost in thoroughly cleaning out the show cages and traveling cases. If for any reason they cannot be attended to at once, they should never be left about in the birdroom itself while awaiting treatment.

DISEASES

Technically the word 'disease' implies any deviation from normal health, whether in the nature of some minor ailment or a serious one resulting in death. Little understood to this day, the diseases of cage birds and their cures are still frequently quoted from some of the standard Victorian authorities who had worked out by trial and error the most effective remedies, often on the basis of human ailments and their treatment. In the highly commercialized world of poultry keeping however, a great deal of research has been carried out in recent years upon the subject of disease, and it is possible that many of the ailments of the domestic fowl may have their counterparts in the canary, although those induced by the intensive conditions under which poultry are housed are unlikely to be encountered in the ordinary way, neither, of course, are those which are known to be peculiar to gallinaceous birds.

Any fancier who is particularly interested is advised to consult a technical work on the subject, where he will probably find that the diseases have been classified according to the sources of infection such as bacteria, viruses, protozoa, parasites or fungi, and then sub-divided according to whether they are infectious or non-infectious, contagious or non-contagious. Methods of their dissemination may be discussed and this will be followed by full descriptions of various symptoms, methods of diagnosis and then the recommended treatment for each complaint.

For the practical fancier however, such pathological detail is irrelevant, his only interest being in a quick and efficient cure should any ailment become manifest. For this purpose the more commonly encountered troubles can be conveniently divided into two categories, (a) those affecting the respiratory system and (b) those affecting the digestive system and, since it is frequently impossible to diagnose accurately from which particular complaint within either group a bird may be suffering, a standard method of primary treatment for each is often the simplest course to adopt.

Respiratory Diseases: These may range from a temporary loss of voice due to a cold or chill, to asthma, bronchitis, catarrh and pneumonia. In all cases there is some inflammation of the respiratory tract differing only in its nature, severity and location, which may be anywhere from the nostrils to the lungs themselves. The most obvious symptom to be noted in all these complaints is the difficulty in breathing, which is often accompanied by a certain amount of wheezing according to the nature of the attack. This becomes especially noticeable if the bird is compelled to fly about the cage for a few seconds, when it will become particularly distressed in attempting to recover its breath after the physical effort involved. Birds with respiratory troubles are also fairly easily located at night by means of their labored and wheezy breathing, and if any doubt is felt about the health of a bird a visit to the birdroom after dark will frequently settle the matter.

Mild cases can be treated by giving the bird a little bread and milk, to which three or four drops of cod liver oil emulsion have been added, sprinkled with sugar and a few grains of maw seed. This should be continued for a few days, and at the same time fifteen drops of glycerine, honey and lemon juice should be added to the drinking water daily. This simple treatment may at least relieve the distress of the bird, and if the case is a minor one a permanent cure may be effected. However, a more serious condition will need the administration of drugs.

Medicines for birds are marketed by some firms of veterinary chemists and are obtainable through the usual fanciers' suppliers, and possibly the best course would be to purchase these and to follow the manufacturers' directions. Actually many of the patent medicines supplied for coughs, colds, bronchitis and so on can be used effectively, although the exact dosage for birds is always something of a hit and miss affair, but a reasonable amount for a trial would be about 15 to 20 drops in the normal drinker of water.

Nearly all of these complaints are induced by bad housing conditions. Damp, drafts, fluctuating temperatures and above all inadequate ventilation are the main causes, so that avoidance of trouble is clearly in the hands of the fancier.

Other infections of the respiratory tract are known and may be brought about either by the presence of fungi or parasites. In these cases also there is the usual difficulty in breathing, together with sneezing and spluttering as if in an attempt to expel some obstruction in the throat. A common fungus infection is known as *aspergillosis*, the spores of which are to be found in many organic substances which may have become moldy. If the birds are exposed to such materials these spores are easily inhaled and develop in the air passages and lungs. There is no known cure at present, and death usually results fairly rapidly. Prevention is a matter of avoiding the use of suspect seed or an unsuitable type of floor covering which might harbor the fungus.

A parasite that occasionally invades the trachea is sometimes known as the 'gapeworm' on account of the effect it produces in the victim. Eggs or newly hatched larvae that have been coughed up by an infected bird may be accidentally picked up by others, and can be readily passed from beak to beak in the act of feeding, either between a mated pair or from parents to young, and thus, to avoid spreading the trouble, the necessity for isolation is obvious. In effecting a cure a fair measure of success has recently been achieved by the use of anti-mite aerosol sprays. If one or two squirts from the canister are directed inside the cage and it is then quickly covered with a cloth for a few minutes, the sufferer will be compelled to inhale the tiny droplets. This can be repeated three or four times daily until relief has occurred.

Digestive Diseases: Disorders of the alimentary tract include constipation, diarrhea, dysentery, enteritis, indigestion and congestion of the liver, although some of these should more properly be termed 'symptoms' rather than 'complaints' in themselves. In all cases there is inflammation of the lining of the digestive tract at some point which may prevent its proper functioning. In severe cases this may result in failure to assimilate the food properly, which could lead to malnutrition and death. Affected birds become listless, dull of eye and 'thick', with the feathers all puffed out. They often sleep for a good deal of the time, waking briefly to pay visits to the seed and water vessels and being obviously in some pain and distress.

The causes of the irritation may be many, but they are almost always introduced through some errors in feeding such as stale or sour food, unwashed greenstuff that may have been contaminated by animals, or lack of cleanliness in food or water vessels. The trouble may often be prevented from developing into anything more serious by giving a mild aperient in the early stages to ensure that the offending material has been removed from the system, and then feeding a little bread and milk dusted with powdered bismuth and sprinkled with maw seed. Warmth is usually beneficial in the treatment of intestinal disorders so that removal to the house, or hospital cage if possible, would hasten recovery.

If no improvement is effected fairly quickly by these simple remedies, one of the proprietary medicines prepared by the veterinary chemists should be made use of, as advised in the preceding section.

Other Troubles: Not associated either with respiratory or digestive organs are such items as continuous molt ('soft molt'), sore feet, slipped claws, and physical accidents such as broken legs or wings, but most of these are rare in well-managed birdrooms.

DEALING WITH SICK BIRDS

Although caring for sick birds seems to have a kind of fascination for some people, the majority of fanciers want as little to do with them as possible, their aim sensibly being to have a vigorous and healthy stock and not a roomful of semi-invalids. If this premise is accepted it must first be decided whether in fact it is worth while bothering with a sick bird at all, and in many cases it will be found that the wisest course is to be quite firm and destroy any that fail to make a reasonably quick recovery under treatment.

Prompt action is essential when dealing with disease, and as soon as a bird is observed to be showing signs of illness it should be isolated from the remainder, to prevent any possible dissemination of germs among them, and its cage should be cleaned out and disinfected as soon as possible. Many fanciers keep a special hospital cage for emergencies, which is provided with a glass front and often has a small heating element beneath the floor as a means of keeping the cage warm. Such cages are obtainable from the manufacturers or can be constructed by a reasonably handy man, using a 60-watt domestic light bulb as a source of heat. If a comfortable temperature of about 70° to 80° F. can be maintained it will be sufficient in most cases, and a thermometer fixed inside the cage will enable this to be carefully watched and regulated accordingly.

The floor of the hospital cage should always be covered with clean white blotting paper, not only for its absorbent properties, but to allow for observation of the condition of the bowels, and any medicines prescribed should be given in glass vessels and not metal or plastic ones. As a general rule drugs should rarely be continued over a long period, especially in the case of laxatives.

PARASITES

Many species of external parasites are known to infest birds in general, but fortunately for the canary breeder two only are likely to be encountered in the ordinary way. Even these need never present any serious problem, and under conditions of good management and sanitation they can be completely eliminated. Many fanciers in fact make it a matter of personal pride that these pests are unknown in their birdrooms.

Red Mite: Although actually grey in color these mites usually appear red because they so often contain the blood of the birds on which they have been feeding and, since they are blood-sucking creatures, they can obviously become a menace when present in large numbers. They are 'intermittent' parasites which come out to feed on the birds at night and then hide away in cracks and crevices during the day, and because of this habit, and their rapid reproductive cycle under warm conditions, a severe infestation may easily build up during the summer months unless a constant watch is kept. At this period the entire process from egg to adult takes only about a week to complete, but during cold weather they do not reproduce to any extent.

Their presence is easily discovered by examining likely hiding places such as the ends of perches, corners of cages, undersides of sand trays and joints in the woodwork supporting the cages, and a visit to the birdroom at night will reveal a constant restlessness and irritation among the birds, while in the light of a torch the parasites may be seen moving about the cages.

They are not difficult to destroy if they can be reached with a contact type of insecticide, but there is always the problem of getting the material deep into their hiding places. Various anti-mite sprays are on the market in aerosol form and these provide the fancier with the most convenient method of dealing with the pest, but an equally effective treatment is to paint all the likely cracks and crevices of the cages with a solution made from camphor dissolved in turpentine or paraffin. In severe cases of infestation the roof, side walls, joints and even floor boards of the birdroom may have to be treated, to ensure complete eradication.

The pest may be introduced by allowing cages, traveling cases, or bird boxes from questionable sources to remain lying about in the birdroom, or occasionally by birds themselves, since it is possible for a few mites to remain on them during the day. Clean, dry, well-ventilated birdrooms, built to admit plenty of sunshine, are less likely to become seriously infested than are damp, dirty, dark places; so the inference regarding good housing is obvious.

Body Lice: These are small greyish insects, about one tenth of an inch in length, which are permanent parasites, spending their entire life cycle upon the body of the bird and only leaving it in order to transfer to another host. They are not blood-sucking parasites like the red mite but feed mainly upon skin and feather tissue, thereby causing considerable irritation and annoyance to the birds on which they live. Their presence results ultimately in loss of condition among the birds, and in cases of severe infestation feathers may be lost due to their quills having been gnawed away at skin level.

Birds infested with lice are constantly pecking and scratching at their plumage, particularly around the neck, and shaking their feathers in an effort to dislodge the pests. If the bird is examined in the hand and the feathers blown aside the insects may be seen running over the skin and among the underflue in an attempt to get out of sight.

Since lice are permanent parasites it is clear that any method of control must involve treating the birds themselves, in order to bring the insecticide into contact with the pest. Hand-washing as though preparing the bird for exhibition has sometimes been recommended, but unless a suitable insecticide is included in the water it is unlikely to be completely satisfactory. The more usual method of treatment is dusting the birds with an insecticidal powder of which several are on the market, and if properly carried out this is generally effective.

The bird should be held gently but firmly and the powder applied well down among the underflue, using a container with a perforated top. The 'pinch method' can also be used, in which a small amount of powder is applied by the thumb and forefinger to each part of the body in turn, special attention being given to the back of the neck, the thighs and under the wings. Another useful method is to use a 'dusting bag' in which a small muslin or plastic bag has a corner cut away, sufficiently large to allow the bird's head to be thrust through. The bird is then placed in the bag with its head protruding through the hole and a liberal quantity of dusting powder shaken inside. It is allowed to flutter its wings but is prevented from withdrawing its head into the bag, which thus safeguards the eyes from being irritated by the powder.

After any of these dusting treatments the birds are returned to clean cages, but since none of the materials at present in use for the destruction of lice is effective against the eggs, a second application will usually be necessary after an interval of about ten days to destroy any subsequent hatchings.

DISINFECTION

Occasions may sometimes arise in which it is thought desirable to disinfect the birdroom as a whole, in which case fumigation may be resorted to, using a method frequently adopted by broiler producers between batches of birds. This involves the use of *formaldehyde vapor*, which is generated by pouring formalin upon crystals of permanganate of potash, the quantities required being 1½ fluid ounces of formalin and ¾ ounce of potassium permanganate for every 100 cubic feet of air space. Before commencing, the birdroom must be emptied of birds and then all windows and ventilators closed to seal the room. Since a fair amount of heat is generated by the chemical action, a metal basin or similar container should be placed on a piece of slate upon the floor and then the required amount of potassium permanganate placed in the basin and the formalin poured on. The door is then closed and left for 12 hours, after which the vapor should be allowed to disperse and the room thoroughly ventilated and cleaned before returning the birds.

This procedure is usually effective against most insect pests and other organisms such as bacteria and fungi. The use of special vapor generators such as are employed in the fumigation of greenhouses should *not* be contemplated, as these are generally based upon the insecticide B.H.C. which leaves a deposit that would be highly toxic to birds.

For the cleansing of individual cages a thorough washing out with a solution containing any of the well-known household disinfectants is usually sufficient, provided that care is taken first to remove all dirt and debris so that it can penetrate all joints and corners. Furthermore, disinfectants should always be used at their recommended strength otherwise they may not be fully effective.

ADDITIONAL READING

For the fancier who may wish to have a book of reference on hand for the diagnosis and treatment of diseases the classic work is *Stroud's Digest on the Diseases of Birds* which, although not completely up-to-date since the introduction of the more recent antibiotics, has the merit of having been written by one who spent many years of practical research into the diseases of birds. A current publication, *Bird Diseases*, by Drs. L. Arnall and I. Keymer is available with the latest methods of treatment, including some of the simpler surgical procedures. Both books are published and distributed by T.F.H. Publications, Inc., Neptune City, N.J.

VARIETIES

10
Color and Markings

It is desirable that the beginner in the canary fancy should become familiar as soon as possible with the basic colors common to all breeds, and with the recognition of the whole range of markings and variegation that are technically accepted by fanciers. Such knowledge is essential both from the point of view of the proper selection of his breeding pairs, and from the necessity of making correct entries at shows.

The old established conception among members of the non-fancying public of the canary as being only of a plain yellow color has largely disappeared, and it is now generally appreciated that even the most elegant highly-bred exhibition bird can have exactly the same coloring as an ordinary wild canary without detracting from its value. This wild-type of plumage coloration is known to fanciers as 'self green'.

Between the clear yellow canary on the one hand and the self green on the other there are many intermediate types, known as variegated birds, the diverse markings of which form not only a basis for classification but provide a simple accurate description of birds that is well understood between fanciers.

BASIC PIGMENTS

The pigments involved in giving color to the plumage of the canary are derived from the food eaten by the bird and are deposited in the feathers as they are developing at molting time. They are three only in number namely yellow, black and brown, and various combinations of these give rise to the different color types about to be described. Birds of the Red Factor series however, have an additional pigment, that of red, and details of this will be given under the appropriate chapter' heading.

Yellow: The basic yellow coloring of the canary, which is known as 'lipochrome', is derived from certain carotenoid substances in the bird's diet such as greenstuff, egg yolk and some seeds, and is a fat soluble pigment which becomes deposited fairly evenly throughout the whole of the body feathering. Exceptions are to be found in the 'underflue', the soft fluffy part of the feather next to the bird's body, and in large flight feathers of the wings and the tail which are mainly white with only an edging of yellow.

The yellow lipochrome thus forms a basic ground color to the plumage upon which other pigments may, or may not, be superimposed.

The actual shade of the coloring can vary considerably and may range from a brilliant dandelion yellow in some individuals to a pale lemon in others. This is partly a matter of sex, as cock birds are by nature more brightly colored than the hens, but is also controlled by heredity and feeding, and poorly colored birds of either sex can occur in any breed.

In varieties that are normally color fed for exhibition purposes the ground color can be temporarily changed from yellow to some shade of orange, which might vary from glowing tangerine to a pale apricot, according to the sex and natural coloring of the bird before color feeding, and details of this process were discussed in the chapter dealing with molting.

Black and Brown: The two dark pigments are known as 'melanins' and are formed by the bird from proteins in its diet. They are deposited in the form of minute granules in the cells of the feathers and are by no means evenly distributed all over the body, even in the case of the self green. In this type of bird many different shades of coloring can be distinguished. Certain areas of the body may be distinctly bright green, others a duller green, and still others verging on bronze, while the wing and tail feathers and the central shafts of the body feathers are practically black. Although unaffected by the lipochrome, the underflue is colored by melanin and is usually dark grey.

These varying colors are the visible result of the dark pigments being superimposed to a greater or lesser extent upon the yellow ground color, but if the black pigment is lacking and only brown remains we have instead of a self green the easily recognizable mutant form known as the self cinnamon.

It should be noted that the melanin pigments also affect the color of the eye, so that even clear yellow birds can be distinguished as being of green or cinnamon 'blood'. In greens they are known as 'dark-eyed' birds and in cinnamons as 'pink-eyed'. The latter name is not a particularly accurate description as it is only in the nestling that the eye looks at all pink; in the adult bird it is so dark a brown as to appear very little different from that of the dark-eyed bird except in a good light.

VARIEGATION

The condition in which the dark pigments of the canary's plumage are confined to certain areas of the body while others remain unpigmented except by lipochrome, is technically known to fanciers as 'variegation'.

The actual disposition of the dark areas is governed by quite a different group of genes from those responsible for the production of color pigment as such, and they are commonly referred to as 'variegation factors'. In other words, one set of factors decides what colors the bird may be *capable* of exhibiting but quite another set determines whether or not these colors *shall* be exhibited. The dark plumaged self green or self cinnamon birds both have a complete set of variegation factors, while in the completely clear bird, although it possesses genes for the production of melanin pigment, all variegation factors have been suppressed. The variegated birds represent various intermediate stages between these two extremes.

Apart from these variegation factors there is probably an allied group of *pattern* factors which operate in controlling the actual areas of the body over which variegation shall occur. So far little genetical research has been done in this direction, although a good working knowledge of the subject must have been in the hands of the old-time fanciers who specialized in the production of evenly marked birds.

From a practical point of view, the following sub-divisions are generally recognized in the classification of most breeds of canary:

Clear: No dark feathering apparent at all. Very rarely some otherwise clear birds possess a certain amount of dark pigment on the underflue, but provided it does not show on the surface as the bird stands on the perch, it is generally accepted as clear.

Ticked: Specialist societies differ somewhat in their definition of what constitutes a ticked bird but, generally speaking, a tick is a single small area of dark feathers (¾ of an inch in diameter) appearing anywhere on the body, or one wing or tail mark consisting of not more than three adjacent dark feathers which thus form a single dark mark.

Variegated: The whole range of birds whose plumage is more or less irregularly marked with light and dark areas. Fanciers frequently sub-divide this class of bird into lightly variegated, in which less than half of the plumage is dark, and heavily variegated, in which more than half of the feathering is dark. In the case of the Border Fancy canary, a very heavily variegated form known as 'three parts dark' is also catered for in the classification.

Foul: The foul marked bird is the dark counterpart of a ticked bird and thus the reverse definition applies. It is an otherwise dark bird which has a single patch of light feathers (¾ of an inch in diameter) anywhere on the body, or light feathers not exceeding three in number in a wing or tail. Once again there is some disparity among specialist societies, and some authorities will accept any number of light feathers in the wings or tail provided there are none on the body.

Self: This term is applied to birds in which the dark pigments are solid throughout with no light feathering showing anywhere in any part of the body, wings or tail.

TECHNICAL MARKINGS

At one time evenly marked birds, as distinct from the general run of irregularly marked, variegated specimens, were much admired and a great deal of time and patience was given by fanciers in their production. In these, the areas of variegation have been limited to three places only—the eyes, the secondary flight feathers on the wings and the outer tail feathers—and although of less importance nowadays they are still recognized by special technical terms. It is rare however, for them to be given separate classes at shows, and they usually compete with the variegated birds.

Six Pointed: An evenly marked bird with all six marks present, namely each eye, both wings and each side of the tail.

Four Pointed: A bird possessing four of the technical marks in any combination, e.g. both eyes and both wings, both wings and outer tail feathers or both eyes and outer tail feathers. The most popular of these, and certainly the most attractive, is the first.

Two Pointed: A bird having only two technical marks, generally the two wing points.

BUFF

In describing the basic yellow ground color of the canary it was stated that the lipochrome pigment responsible for this extended fairly evenly throughout the body feathering, but this must now be qualified by saying that an important exception occurs in the case of the group of birds known to fanciers as 'buffs'. In these birds the pigment stops just short of the outer margin of the web of each feather, leaving a thin edging of white, and the general effect of this is to produce a slightly frosted or mealy appearance upon the yellow, which is particularly easy to distinguish in the region of the head and neck where the feathers are smaller and more closely placed together.

Apart from the frosting there is also some reduction in the intensity of the yellow pigment, so that buff birds always

145

appear slightly paler than their yellow counterparts. In addition there are some minor structural differences in the feather, those of the buffs being a little larger, broader and somewhat softer in texture than those of the yellows, with the result that the buff bird tends to present a rather more bulky appearance.

In the case of dark pigmented birds the buff is recognized by a greyish or silvery edging to the feather, as it is only the yellow lipochrome that is affected by this particular phenomenon. All that has already been said concerning the melanin pigments and the variegation and pattern factors applies equally to both yellow and buff canaries.

Feather structure. Feathers taken from the same part of the body of a yellow (left) and a buff (right) Border Fancy canary.

WHITE VARIETIES

Although we have been mainly concerned so far with canaries possessing a yellow ground color there are also in existence white ground canaries, in which the lipochrome has either been suppressed or is lacking.

Actually, white canaries were known as long ago as the eighteenth century and were listed among the 29 'varieties' of Hervieux, but apparently they were allowed to die out. Occasionally writers have made mention of them but it was not until the present century that they have made their undisputed re-appearance and have become safely established. There are, in fact, two distinct white mutations now in existence—the 'dominant' and the 'recessive' white. The latter is still relatively uncommon and is mainly of interest only to experimental breeders, but the dominant white has been introduced into most of the standard breeds of today although its popularity has remained rather limited.

The only difference between the yellow and white canary that need concern us here is that of their ground color. The melanins and the variegation factors are the same in each group and they are classified in the same way. The effect of the black and brown pigments upon the white ground color however is that, instead of green being produced, the dark color appears as a slate-blue, and in place of cinnamon the brown pigment appears as fawn. Such birds are usually referred to as 'self blue' or 'self fawn'.

AGE DIFFERENCES

It is an almost impossible task to assess a bird's age accurately, so that when purchasing his initial stock the beginner is forced to rely upon the integrity of the fancier from whom he is obtaining the birds. Very old canaries however, are readily recognized by their less sleek appearance with rougher duller plumage, their more lethargic manner and in particular by the condition of their legs and feet, which become distinctly more scaly with the advance of age.

When young canaries leave the nest they are completely clothed with a set of feathers that will last them until their first molt begins, at the age of about eight to twelve weeks.

At this stage they are said to be in 'nest feather' plumage. During their first adult molt the whole body feathers are renewed, but *not* the wing and tail feathers. The birds are then known as 'unflighted'. At the following year's molt the complete set of feathers are replaced, including the wings and tail, and the bird then becomes 'flighted'. This process is repeated at each successive molt.

Quite simply then, a 'nest feather' bird is a youngster before its first molt, an 'unflighted' bird is one in the year following its first molt, and a 'flighted' bird is one that is over one year old, having undergone a second molt. Some fanciers in fact refer to these as 'overyear' birds.

SEXING

Unlike some species of birds, in canaries the outward visible differences between sexes are not very well marked and can really only be discerned by the practiced eye of the fancier who has had plenty of experience in the observation of these matters. Even here, few would lay claim to one hundred per cent infallibility.

In general a cock bird has a bolder, more jaunty carriage of the body than the hen, with a fuller eye and brighter coloring about the forehead, face and throat. His call note usually has a louder and more confident ring about it than that of the hen.

The only really satisfactory proof of sex however, until the breeding season comes around, is the song, although even here the novice can sometimes be deceived by the fact that some hens are capable of uttering a sort of sustained twittering that might be mistaken for the song of a very young cock bird. It is really quite different however, from the loud, full-throated singing of an adult cock, which is often accompanied by a swaying of the body from side to side during delivery.

When the birds are in breeding condition the difference between the sexes is easy to ascertain by an examination of the vent areas. Birds have no distinctly different external sexual organs as do mammals, but if the feathers of the abdomen are blown aside, the vent of a cock bird in breeding condition is quite prominent and somewhat pointed while that of the hen is rounder and flatter and not so much raised above the general level of the abdomen. It must again be emphasized that this difference is only apparent in birds in full breeding condition—out of season the organ shows no differentiation and one can only rely upon the song as a certain guide to sex.

After reading the contents of this chapter the beginner may perhaps be excused for feeling some bewilderment at the multiplicity of colors, markings, variegation and so on, that are to be found among canaries. It is however, important basic knowledge that, once mastered, will enable him to enter freely into conversation with his fellow fanciers without the slightest dismay at references to such things as 'clear yellow unflighted cocks', 'heavily variegated flighted buff hens', 'foul greens' or 'evenly marked cinnamons'. Not only will he have a clear mental picture of any bird that is under discussion, but also an underlying knowledge of the principles involved if it comes to a detailed analysis of any point that may be raised.

11

The Border Fancy

HISTORY

Many breeders of the most popular canary of today, the Border Fancy, might perhaps be a little surprised to learn that none of the great Victorian authorities on cage birds, many of whom produced comprehensive books on the subject, made any mention whatsoever of this variety. Indeed it was not until the third edition of Wallace's *The Canary Book*, published in 1893, that the author, in his preface, stated that he had revised and brought his book completely up to date, which involved among other things, the inclusion of 'particulars of the variety now known as the Border Fancy'.

An earlier reference to the breed however, had been made in *The British Canary*, by C.A. House (1889), using its older title of the 'Cumberland Fancy,' and this probably constitutes the very first mention of the variety in the literature of the canary fancy. This does not necessarily mean of course that canaries of the Border type had not existed before this date, for almost certainly they had, and probably for a very long time.

In the later book of his, *Canaries*, (1923), House explained that in those early days classes used to be given at several of the shows in Cumberland, Westmorland, and the South of Scotland for 'Common Canaries'. They were usually filled with birds of no particular type, that is to say, none of the currently recognized breeds, and prizes were awarded mainly for color and feather quality. Sometime during the 'eighties the breeders of Cumberland evidently started to call these birds by the name of their own county, but in the border counties of Scotland and elsewhere, where birds of a similar type were bred, they continued to be known simply as Common Canaries.

Each side of the border laid claim to being the birthplace of the original breed, but to the men of the north must go the credit for first getting it organized on a proper basis. An inaugural meeting was held in 1890 at Hawick, when a resolution was passed disapproving of the existing names and declaring that from then on the bird should be known as the 'Border Fancy Canary'. A specialist club was immediately formed under the title of 'The Border Fancy Canary Club,' and the Scottish influence on the breed during its early history can be gauged from the fact that all of the leading officials up to the first World War, and even for some time afterwards, were Scots.

The membership of the newly formed club was just 43, but today, with sixteen additional specialist societies to its name in Great Britain alone, the number of breeders of this robust and successful variety runs into many thousands. There are two Border Canary associations now functioning in the United States, and all state and local shows bench a goodly number of Border entries.

The following year a special meeting was held to select a model from among the leading birds of the season, and for many years a portrayal of the individual chosen was contained in the book of rules, as a guide for breeders. The Border of those days became affectionately known to fanciers as the 'wee gem,' in direct reference to its size and brilliance, and it has not been until comparatively recent times that it has undergone any great change.

In the years immediately following the second World War many very large, so-called 'Borders' began to appear on the show-benches which, not only by their size but by many bodily characteristics also, betrayed the fact that they had Norwich blood in their veins. Unfortunately some judges saw fit to award prizes to these birds, and as a result a trend was set for a time in which the neat appearance and jaunty carriage so essential to a good Border were in danger of disappearing. Subsequently a reaction set in against the larger, coarser bird, and during the period of refinement that followed, a more compact, rounder type of Border has emerged, differing in slight detail from the original conception of the breed.

DESCRIPTION

The essential characteristics of the Border Fancy can be summed up by the words 'type' and 'quality'. In general appearance it immediately gives the impression of complete symmetry, with no one feature predominating to the exclusion of another so that a perfect balance of outline is maintained throughout. It is a sprightly, active bird, rather lightly built and with a gay and jaunty carriage of the body. It has close and compact feathering showing no tendency whatever to coarseness, so that all its features appear cleanly cut with flowing, harmonious lines.

The head is neat and nicely rounded with a bright, alert eye centrally placed and a fine, smallish beak. The neck is well proportioned in relation to head and body and should never be too thick nor too fine, either of which would destroy the whole effect. The body gives an impression of roundness when seen in cross section and, after a gentle curve over the shoulders, the back gradually tapers off in a straight line towards the root of the tail. The breast also is gracefully rounded, yet without any undue prominence, and again tapers off cleanly between the legs to the underside of the tail producing, along with the line of the back, a perfect wedge shape.

The feathers of the tail are closely compacted, continuing exactly the line of the wedge, for if carried too high or too low the whole balance of the bird's appearance would obviously be upset. The wings are compact and carried tightly-braced and close to the body, with the tips of the primary flight feathers just meeting each other—never overlapping, crossing or failing to meet, which would leave the rump feathers exposed.

In keeping with the general conformation of the bird, the legs are of moderate length and show practically nothing of the thigh joint, while the natural carriage of the body is in a semi-erect position at an angle of approximately 60 degrees.

Size has sometimes been a matter of contention with Border fanciers, but undoubtedly the over large ones have had their day and are no longer being tolerated, either by the specialist judges or the leading breeders. The rules of the Border Fancy societies specifically lay down that the length must not exceed 5½ inches.

Apart from its beautiful balanced proportions, perhaps the most admired feature of this canary is its superb feather quality, the plumage of a really good specimen being close, firm and fine, presenting a smooth, well-groomed appearance almost as if it were carved out of wax. It must be appreciated of course that type and quality are interdependent aspects of the whole picture, since poor feather quality will almost invariably spoil the outline of an otherwise good bird and conversely, perfect feather quality cannot rescue from mediocrity a bird that is badly put together.

From the very inception of the breed color feeding with red color food was frowned upon, and a decision to debar its use was made after a plebiscite of members in 1901, and to this day the Border is one of the breeds of canary still shown in natural color. Possibly this fact, together with its lively disposition and the very freedom with which it breeds, has in some way contributed to its widespread popularity.

BREEDING

In the breeding of Border Fancies, as indeed with all other varieties, it is essential to be thoroughly conversant with the standard required and to have an accurate and unbiased eye when selecting the pairs. Wise fanciers spend a good deal of time in matching up their breeding stock, often running them into show cages in order to study them point by point, and frequently referring to the pedigree book if any matter should be in doubt. It is always advisable to be somewhat over-critical rather than too tolerant, since the tendency for faults to be perpetuated is only too well known among breeders.

As the very disposition of the Border is to be alert, sprightly and active, one of the worst errors is to breed from birds that show any tendency to be coarse and heavily built. Not only are they inclined to be sluggish and awkward in

Young Border Fancy chicks three weeks old and just leaving the nest.

action, but they nearly always have faulty carriage of the body, usually being too much across the perch instead of at the desired angle of 60 degrees. Coarseness is also exhibited in various details such as large beaks, flat heads and thick necks, all of which should be assiduously guarded against.

The importance of good feather quality has already been sufficiently emphasized, but it is surprising how often this is overlooked. The really bad specimen of course is readily detected, but poor feather quality is often betrayed in smaller ways, by any suggestion of 'eyebrows,' by looseness at the thighs and vent, and by too lengthy flight and tail feathers, which are frequently indicative of overlong body feathering too.

Even the most inexperienced breeder would not hesitate in rejecting a bird possessing all of the faults so far listed, but it should be his endeavor to prevent the intrusion of any of them into his stock, and therefore he should be very circumspect in accepting for breeding any bird possessing a fault to any marked degree. There are so many high quality Borders available that it is quite unnecessary to have to make do with mediocre ones.

The Border Fancy exists in all of the usual standard canary colors, but in every case, whatever the color it is essential for it to be bright and level throughout, with no suggestion of unevenness or dullness, and showing a distinctly glossy sheen which signifies vigorous condition and high quality. For the fanciers with a limited stock it is perhaps advisable to mate a clear to a variegated bird in most of his breeding pairs, with the object of providing suitable material for the various classes scheduled at the shows; but some may wish to specialize in clears, greens, cinnamons or whites, any of which can prove quite rewarding.

A nice brood of young Border Fancies at eight weeks of age.

It has often been stated with regard to color that green or heavily variegated birds must constantly be used to maintain depth of tone, but this, in fact, is quite unnecessary and many clear strains have been bred true for generations without recourse to any dark blood. Careful selection of well-colored stock is the real essential in this respect, and the mere fact of using a green or variegated bird does not in itself enhance the color value of the subsequent youngsters.

With this breed, more perhaps than any other, it is advisable for the novice to adhere rigidly to the normal yellow x buff mating, owing to the known tendency for double buffing to produce somewhat thicker, heavier-feathered birds, and double yellowing to result in slimmer, rather more 'racy' types. The expert however, may occasionally depart from the standard practice if, as a result of his experience, he finds it necessary to do so to correct some incipient fault.

MOLTING

Although the Border breeder is relieved of the necessity of color feeding his birds for exhibition purposes, he can and should take every possible step to ensure that they are able to realize their full potential *natural* color during the molt. Reference to the chapter on molting will reveal that this can best be achieved by the use of many different species of wild seeds, and more particularly by an abundant supply of dark green leaves, such as those of spinach and kale, which contain high proportions of lutein which is essential for the formation of yellow pigment in the plumage of the canary. Other food items with a high yield of this substance are yolk of egg and rape seed, both of which can therefore be included with advantage at this period of the year.

EXHIBITING

Not only is the Border the most commonly kept variety of canary at the present time but also the most widely exhibited, and at shows of any standing competition is usually quite severe. To be successful therefore, the fancier should leave nothing to chance and ensure that his birds reach the showbench with everything in their favor. This will include scrupulous attention to details appertaining to the showcage and its fittings, as laid down by the specialist societies, as well as the careful training of the birds themselves so that they come before the judge at the very peak of their form.

In the general chapter on exhibiting the elements of training were dealt with, but in addition to these it is essential for the Border to have a free and sprightly 'action'. A really good mover should hop from perch to perch readily and with confidence, unassisted by any flip of the wings nor showing any unsteadiness in balance at the completion of each hop. It is important to train the bird to remain happily on the perches and show no inclination to jump around on the bottom of the cage nor climb upon the wires, but always to be something of a showman with a certain amount of 'swank,' almost as if inviting the attention of the judge.

The standard show cage for Borders is known as the 'Dewar' pattern, and is entirely painted black. With the exception of the wooden base it is an all wire construction with a 3-wire sliding door at one end. It is rectangular in shape, being 12¼ inches long and 4 9/16 inches wide, but has a rounded top with the height of the curve being 11¼ inches at the center and 9¼ inches at the sides. At the opposite end to the door a seed trough is provided at floor level, which is partially covered but has a slot cut in it to allow access to the seed. Some cages have a small drawer fitted inside this trough. The perches are 5/8 inch in diameter and are spirally turned with sixteen teeth, and no other type of perch is permitted at shows covered by specialist club patronage. The small sized glass drinkers are fixed by means of a wire ring opposite the end of the left-hand perch. On the bottom of the cage oat husks only are allowed as a floor covering, and the label with class and cage number must be placed directly under the perch opposite to the drinker. Any subsequent award labels will be fixed immediately to the left of the class label.

Prohibited details of the show cage are round drinker holes, white or brass knobs to the seed drawer and holes instead of a slot in the cover of the seed trough. Failure to observe these seemingly minor points may debar an exhibitor from competing for specialist club awards, so that it is in the best interest of the newcomer to ensure that he is correct in every detail in his show cages when he either makes or purchases them for the first time.

OFFICIAL STANDARD

The following is the official description of the ideal bird as laid down by the Border Fancy Canary Club.

STANDARD OF EXCELLENCE

The grand essentials of a Border Fancy Canary are type and quality. Without these it is useless.

The general appearance is that of a clean-cut, lightly-made, compact, proportionable, close-feathered canary, showing no tendency to heaviness, roughness or dullness, but giving the impression of fine quality and symmetry throughout.

HEAD (10 points): Small, round and neat-looking; beak fine; eyes central to roundness of head and body.

BODY (15 points): Back well filled and nicely rounded, running in almost a straight line from a gentle rise over the shoulders to the point of the tail. Chest also nicely rounded, but neither heavy nor prominent, the line gradually tapering to the vent.

WINGS (10 points): Compact and carried close to the body, just meeting at tips, a little lower than the root of the tail.

LEGS (5 points): Of medium length, showing little thigh, fine and in harmony with the other points, yet corresponding.

PLUMAGE (10 points): Close, firm, fine in quality, presenting a smooth, glossy, silken appearance, free from frill or roughness.

TAIL (5 points): Close-packed and narrow, being nicely rounded and filled in at the root.

POSITION (15 points): Semi-erect, standing at an angle of 60 degrees.

CARRIAGE: Gay, jaunty, with full poise of the head.

COLOR (15 points): Rich, soft, and pure, as level in tint as possible throughout, but extreme depth and hardness such as color feeding gives are *debarred*.

HEALTH (10 points): Condition and cleanliness shall have due weight.

SIZE (5 points): *not to exceed 5½ inches* in length.

TOTAL — 100 points

Ticked Birds: A 'ticked' bird shall have only one mark on head or body, wing or tail. Head or body mark to be coverable by a dime, and wing or tail mark not to exceed three dark feathers side by side to form a solid mark. A 'foul' bird shall be the opposite of a 'ticked' bird: Light mark on dark ground.

An Even-marked bird is one with four technical marks, *viz.* both eyes and both wings. A six-pointed bird has dark feathers on each side of the tail in addition to the above marks. Broken eye marks are allowed in even-marked classes, also dark under-fluff. Three part dark birds must be 75 per cent dark.

In judging marked birds 'type and quality' should form the first consideration in these as in other classes, and no prize should be awarded for good marking alone where type does not conform to the club standard.

The Green Border Fancy Canary must conform to the club standard on all points but color. The correct color should be a rich grass green, sound and level throughout, free from bronze or olive tint, pencilling on back to be clear and distinct, but neither broad nor heavy, flank pencilling to be finer but in harmony with that on back. Beak, legs and feet dark; light beaks, legs or feet not to be disqualified, but to count against a bird according to extent. Points to be avoided are: Head too dark, light throat'or thighs, lightness on abdomen towards vent or on rump.

The Cinnamon variety must also conform to the club's standard in all but color. The color to be of rich, deep cinnamon tint throughout, with faint markings on back and flanks. Greenish or too light tints to be avoided.

12

The Yorkshire

HISTORY

Most authorities agree that the Yorkshire Canary is essentially a 'manufactured' breed, created mainly during the last quarter of the nineteenth century from various crosses involving common canaries, the Lancashire Plainhead, the Norwich (old-fashioned type) and the Belgian. In view of all the facts, which have been well documented by those most intimately concerned, this statement of origin must be accepted as true, but it should also be known that Yorkshire had been the home of a particular type of canary for many years previously.

The Rev. Francis Smith mentioned the variety in the 1860's and W.A. Blakston, writing in 1878, stated that it was a breed of ancient date, and went on to say that 'great alteration in style has taken place of late years with respect to this bird and possibly the Yorkshire of today is not precisely the same bird as the Yorkshire of fifty years ago,' a reference which would date it back to the earlier part of the century.

The first examples of the modern Yorkshire were produced by crossing the original common canary of the county with the Lancashire in order to give it size and length, and then, to improve the color and feather quality, the old-style Norwich was introduced. Finally came the idea of slimness and elegance combined with a stylish position, and the Belgian was used to impart these qualities.

With such a mixed ancestry it is little to be wondered at that these early Yorkshires were a somewhat heterogeneous collection and, since even-markings were very much sought after at that time, type was often relegated to second place. Dissatisfaction with this state of affairs led to a series of con-

BORDER FANCY CANARY. This self blue, mated to a self green, would produce greens and blues in equal proportions among their progeny.

ferences being held during the year 1889, which led to the formation of the Yorkshire Union of Ornithological Societies. This was followed in 1894 by the Yorkshire Canary Club, and the drawing up of an official standard towards which ideal the Yorkshire canary was, in future, to be bred.

As a result of this action the variety began to make good progress, and during the first quarter of the present century it rose eventually to the position of the most popular of all exhibition canaries, until overtaken more recently by the Border Fancy. Today, with eleven specialist societies to its credit all over Great Britain, it stands in second place, but is still the most popular breed with overseas fanciers whose requirements provide a steady demand for British-bred stock.

The old standard of perfection called for a long, slim elegant bird and it was often stated, by way of conveying the general impression upon breeders, that the ideal specimen should be capable of passing through a wedding ring! The ideals of breeders do not remain static however, and more recent trends of thought have produced a new model which has now superseded the old standard, and although many of the original characteristics have been retained, the present-day Yorkshire differs in several essentials from the former conception of the breed.

DESCRIPTION

The 'gentleman of the fancy' as it was so often called by earlier writers, is a bird of style and elegance, characteristics which are so evident in a first-class specimen as thoroughly to merit the title, for there should never be anything in its aspect or manner that at any time suggests coarse breeding or slovenliness. It is at the present time the only widely bred representative of a group of varieties known collectively as 'birds of position,' in which a sensitive and nervy action combines with a graceful poise of the body to produce in canaries the equivalent of the thoroughbred in horses.

So important is this position that one quarter of the points allowed are for this feature alone. The desired attitude when the bird is in full pose in its show cage is almost erect, with a confident and dignified carriage of the body. The

Yorkshire should never stand across the perch at a low angle nor show any inclination to crouch, either of which are completely alien to the conception of what the breed should be. The legs are long and straight, yet supple and without any suggestion of stiltiness, and should not show too much of the thigh joint.

Of equal value on the points scale is the feature that every knowledgeable fancier appreciates and recognizes as being the mark of good breeding—namely, feather quality. As in the case of the Border, the feathering is short and close and carried tightly to the body without any suspicion of eyebrow, nor of any roughness or looseness at the thighs or breast, the texture being soft and fine as silk. The wings are long and are carried close to the body, meeting evenly down the center of the back, and the tail also is long and tightly folded, never being wide and spreading, since a loosely folded tail is a blemish which will inevitably spoil the whole balance of an otherwise good Yorkshire.

These characteristics of attitude and feather quality do not differ in any way from the old-time standard, but it is in the 'type' or bodily conformation that the greatest changes have been made in the present-day model of the ideal Yorkshire. Still essentially a long and stylish bird it no longer has the ultra-slim contours of the original type, with the head, neck and shoulders in particular being proportionately larger than in former times.

Instead of being small and round, the head is now officially described as being 'full,' with the back of the skull coming well down towards the rising curve of the shoulders so that there is no appreciable appearance of a neck. The high shoulders are fairly broad and well-rounded, but the main line of the back as viewed from the side is straight and continues so to the root of the tail.

Underneath, and starting just below the beak, the breast is deep and nicely rounded producing, with the rise of the shoulders, a symmetrical outline which then tapers away cleanly between the legs towards the vent and base of the tail, giving a similar wedge shape as was noted in the case of the Border, but in this instance with a much more finely

LANCASHIRE COPPY CANARY. A very old English breed which became extinct during World War II but has recently been re-created
by "breeding back" from stock known to contain Lancashire blood
which had been used for improvement in earlier years.

RED FACTOR CANARY. A melanin pastel red orange cock. Another mutation in which the melanin pigment is diluted and devoid of pencilling.

drawn out taper. The line of the tail however, is not an exact prolongation of the wedge but is carried a little higher, although not so pronounced as to make the bird what is sometimes called 'robin-tailed'.

In section the body is rounded and well filled, never being flat-sided nor having any suggestion of a hollow between the shoulders or running down the back. It has often been represented by writers as giving the appearance of having been turned on a lathe.

The Yorkshire is one of the larger breeds of canary, the average length being about 6¾ inches. It is color-fed for exhibition purposes and although rarely possessing quite so deep a tone as the Norwich, it is important that it should be pure and level throughout the body.

Many years ago a separate race known as 'Liverpool Greens' became associated with the Yorkshire, which they closely resembled in type, so that eventually they were amalgamated and lost their separate identity. As with other varieties of canary however, the green still has a special place in the general classification. Cinnamon blood too is very prevalent throughout the breed, and is said to be the origin of some of the beautiful soft, fine feathering to be found in birds of the highest quality.

BREEDING

The production of high-class Yorkshires has always presented a real challenge to the skill of breeders, a fact that perhaps may be responsible for the somewhat higher prices that good quality stock has commanded, when compared with some other breeds. At no time has this challenge been more in evidence than since the introduction of the present standard when, in the hands of the less skillful fancier, attempts to breed birds with the bolder, fuller 'top end' have often resulted in a number of large, clumsy, coarse-feathered specimens being produced. That these increases in size and feathering have almost always been achieved by double-buff matings should be sufficient to warn the beginner to keep to the general rule of mating yellow to buff, and to leave more adventurous work until greater experience has been gained.

One of the great problems in breeding the Yorkshire is that it is a large breed in which are required the attributes of smartness and high quality more often associated with the smaller varieties. So often it is the smaller bird that has the necessary style and quality, whereas the good-sized specimen frequently lacks these very essential points. Although to be slightly undersized is no great fault in a bird that otherwise has perfect shape and carriage, it is important not to allow any deterioration in this direction to go too far, as it is easier to lose size than to regain it. For this reason many of the old-time authorities recommended that a breeding pair should be made up of a big, lengthy cock bird and a smart, close-feathered, finely-drawn hen. In this way it is certainly possible to correct any coarseness in the cock bird, and to produce among the progeny some at least that will combine type and quality with adequate size. Nevertheless, it may be necessary occasionally to make the mating the other way around, using a neat, typical cock bird paired to a large, bold hen. Although many fanciers of long experience assert that, in general, size and color are inherited from the cock bird and type and quality from the hen, genetically this is unlikely, as experiments involving reciprocal crosses have proved, and matings may be made whichever way round is convenient with every reason to expect equally good results.

Quite apart from the general problem of combining size with quality, there are certain faults of varying degrees of seriousness that the fancier must avoid as far as possible in his breeding pairs. Of these, defective carriage is perhaps the most serious for, as has already been mentioned, any bird that crouches or stands across the perch is diametrically opposed to all that a good Yorkshire should be, and although much can be accomplished in the way of show training, these faults if bred into a strain can never be completely eradicated.

So far as the conformation of the body is concerned the main blemishes are a flat head, which is often accompanied by overhanging eyebrows, a coarse, heavy beak and a hollow neck. A pointed breast, usually associated with twisted or frilled breast feathers, is yet another feature to be avoided, as

RED FACTOR CANARY. Dimorphic hen. Near-white all over but showing intense red coloring on face, wing butts and rump.

YORKSHIRE CANARY. A self green.

also is any bird that is too stout in the waist. This gives the body an almost cylindrical shape with a chopped-off appearance behind the legs, instead of the graceful taper that is needed, and it is usually caused by excessive feather at the waist and thighs.

Long, bare thigh joints are sometimes to be seen in the rather slim, racy birds of the older type, but this is preferable to being too short in the leg which always gives a squat appearance even if the bird otherwise stands well.

Possessing long wings and tail has the effect of accentuating any slight fault in their carriage, and thus great care is again necessary in avoiding the worst of these errors. So far as the wings are concerned, the two extreme defects consist of carrying them too loosely instead of tightly braced, so that they tend to 'fall apart,' thus exposing the lower back and rump, or of having them crossed at the tips with the consequent ugly 'scissor-winged' effect. A hinged tail is also to be avoided, that is, one that is continually dropping out of position instead of being at all times well braced and carried with a just detectable lift.

Finally, from the purely practical point of view in breeding procedure, many Yorkshire fanciers, working on the principle that nothing must at any time induce the birds to adopt a stooping posture, set the perches and nest pans fairly low down in the breeding cages to allow for plenty of head room. Also, on account of the nestlings being rather long and leggy, some breeders favor a somewhat larger and deeper type of nesting receptacle than is normal.

MOLTING

The Yorkshire is a color-fed variety, and reference should be made to this subject in the chapter on molting. Since type, carriage and quality of feather are the major features of the breed, the number of points allowed for color as such are not high on the scale. Nevertheless, every effort should be made to produce as deep and even a tone as is possible, as this may well carry the day in the event of birds competing for top honors which may be of equal merit in other respects.

There is a fairly widespread practice among the fancy of 'tailing' unflighted birds during their first molt—that is to say, pulling out the tail feathers which would not normally be shed at this time. When the new tail grows the feathers are somewhat longer than the original 'baby' ones, so that the bird is thereby given a little extra overall length, hence the object of the exercise. There appears to be no official ruling by the Yorkshire specialist societies either condemning or condoning the practice, but since the effect of color food on the new tail makes the artifice obvious, most judges will merely ignore it and deal with the bird on its merit irrespective of whether it has an 'unnatural' tail or not.

EXHIBITING

Unlike the Border this variety is not required to show movement, so that apart from the perches provided for easy access to the drinker and seed trough, there is only one perch in the show cage upon which the bird should stand alert and straight. Probably no breed requires greater attention nor responds better in the matter of training than the Yorkshire, and leading exhibitors are prepared to spend any amount of time in perfecting their birds for the show bench. As described in the chapter on exhibiting, the fancier should use every possible stratagem to train the bird to stand firm and erect in order to show off its points to full advantage, and frequent handling of the cage becomes very important so that the bird will grip the perch fearlessly and hold itself well while being judged.

The standard show cage is an open wire pattern with a wooden base. The length is 9¼ inches, consisting of 17 wires, and the width is 6¼ inches, with 12 wires. The top is rounded, with an overall height of 14 inches, and the wooden base is 3 1/8 inches deep and made from ¼ inch wood. As with most other show cages, a fairly rigid specification is laid down, departure from which may lead to disqualification. The relevant details are as follows:

Seed trough ¾ inch wide inside, and 1¼ inches deep outside, the top edge to be rounded and to be ¾ inch below the top edge of the cage base. First crossbar

FOUR BREEDS FROM CONTINENTAL EUROPE. 1. The Belgian, with straight back, high shoulders and lowered head. 2. The Dutch Frill, well formed frills on the body but head and neck smooth feathered. 3. The Parisian Frill, tightly curled feathers even extending to the head and neck. 4. The Gibber Italicus, sparse feathering and showing naked thighs and breastbone.   Photos by Mueller-Schmida.

Young canaries — a nest of chicks at about ten days old gaping for food.

6 3/8 inches high from base, second crossbar 10¼ inches high from base. Corner wires and cross wires to be of 14 s.w.g., the other wires to be of 17 s.w.g.

Cages to be fitted with three 5/8 inch x 3/8 inch white oval perches, the two bottom perches to be fixed on the fourth wire from either end of the cage and the top perch to be fixed on the ninth wire from either end of the cage. The perches must be fixed with the bevelled side uppermost and must be oval in section as stated.

All cages to be finished black all over. Zinc or plastic drinkers optional.

The classification of Yorkshire canaries is based on a standard of markings which differs in some respects from that of most other canary societies, so that the novice will need to become conversant with the details in order to enter his birds correctly at the shows. Further complications are presented when he exhibits at shows that are not governed by Yorkshire specialist club rules, where the more usual "universal" classification is likely to apply.

OFFICIAL STANDARD
The following description and scale of points are those laid down by the Yorkshire Canary Club.

SCALE OF POINTS

HEAD (20 points): Full, round and cleanly defined. Backskull deep and carried back in line with rise of shoulders. Eye as near center of head as possible. Shoulders proportionately broad, rounded and carried well up to and gradually merging into the head. Breast full and deep, corresponding to width and rise of shoulders and carried up full to base of beak which should be neat and fine.

BODY (10 points): Well rounded and gradually tapering throughout to tail.

POSITION (25 points): Attitude erect with fearless carriage, legs long without being stilty, and slight lift behind.

FEATHER (25 points): Close, short and tight. Wings proportionately long and evenly carried down the center of the back and firmly set on a compact and closely folded tail.

SIZE (10 points): Length approximately 6¾ inches with corresponding symmetrical proportions.

CONDITION (10 points): Health, cleanliness and sound feathers, color pure and level.

TOTAL — 100 points

STANDARD OF MARKINGS

The presence of dark feather on the thigh or natural discoloration of the beak, legs or feet, or any mark which is not discernible as the bird stands in its natural position in the show cage shall be ignored throughout the whole classification.

Ticked: A ticked bird shall have one mark only, unbroken by any intervening light feather on any part of the body (thighs, legs, beak and feet excluded).

The standards for *Marked Birds* shall be regulated by what are termed technical marks, that is marks on (touching) eyes, flights (primary and/or secondary) and sides of tail. Each eye mark and each tail mark must be distinctly separated from its corresponding mark by a portion of light feathers. A bird which has a cap, or grizzle which touches both eyes is for the purposes of classification considered to have one technical mark only. A bird with a tail consisting of all dark feathers is for the purposes of classification considered to have one technical mark only as there are no intervening light feathers.

Evenly Marked: An evenly marked bird shall have:
1. Two technical marks (both eyes, or flights of both wings, or both sides of tail).
2. Four technical marks (both eyes and flights of both wings, or both eyes and both sides of tail, or flights of both wings and both sides of tail).
3. All six technical marks.

YORKSHIRE CANARY. A deeply forked tail and twisted feathers at the throat are just two of the many faults that would offend the eye of the fancier in this blue variegated white Yorkshire.

BORDER FANCY CANARY. A well rounded and nicely proportioned
yellow cock.

Unevenly Marked: An unevenly marked bird shall have three or five technical markings only.

Variegated Classes: Shall consist of any other variegation not already provided for, i.e.:
1. Lightly variegated, more light than dark.
2. Heavily variegated, more dark than light.

A 'Self' bird is all dark.

A 'Foul' bird has light feathers in wing flights or tail only. The presence of light feathers apart from any wing flights and/or tail feathers would make it a variegated bird.

13
The Norwich

HISTORY

Of all varieties of canary none is better known to the general public, at least by name, than the Norwich, and it has also maintained a higher level of popularity with fanciers over a longer period of time than any other breed. During the Victorian era it was easily the most widely kept variety as is shown, for example, by the entries at the Crystal Palace show of 1870, where in the first two classes alone, which were for clear Norwich canaries, there were no fewer than 125 contestants. Today it may have lost a little ground to the two breeds previously dealt with, but if entries at recent British National Exhibitions can be taken as a reasonable guide, it is at present still our third most popular canary.

There is a generally accepted tradition that it was the Flemish weavers, who settled in Norfolk during the latter part of the sixteenth century, who were responsible for introducing the pastime of canary breeding into East Anglia, but no authoritative information exists in support of this belief. It is a fact however, that canaries have been bred in and around the city of Norwich for a very long time, and by the middle of the nineteenth century the numbers in which they were being raised amounted almost to the proportions of a cottage industry, many thousands of birds being sent annually to the London pet markets. The Norwich is those days in fact seems to have occupied much the same position as the Border does now, being at once the most popular exhibition bird and favorite as a household pet and songster.

Judging from contemporary descriptions and illustrations its similarity to the Border did not end with its popularity, for in appearance too it showed a much greater resem-

NORWICH CANARIES. This pair has been selected by the breeder for the production of exhibition birds. It consists of a clear buff cock bird (left) and a variegated yellow hen (right).

GLOSTER FANCY CANARY. A green corona whose crest radiates
well.

blance to the familiar bird of today than to the modern version of the Norwich canary.

In those days it was essentially a bird of color, no less than 45 points out of 100 being given for this alone and, as if this were not enough, 20 more were allowed for extra sheen and brilliance. With such value being placed on these characteristics it is little to be wondered at that the Norwich canary was the subject of the stormy controversy over color feeding in the 1870's, details of which were given in the chapter on Molting.

From the 1880's onwards such changes took place in the breed as to alter it almost beyond recognition. Only a few years previously, in the late 1870's, the breeders of the Crested Norwich had introduced the massive 'Lancashire Coppy' canary into their stocks with quite astonishing results, and very soon the 'Plainhead' breeders were following their example. By a similar process of almost unlimited outcrossing, either directly with the Lancashire Plainhead, or with the Crest-bred canary which introduced Lancashire blood at second hand, the appearance of the Norwich was altered completely from its original form, and once the craze for size had started, breeders began to concentrate upon this feature alone to the exclusion of other characteristics. It was particularly from such centers of fancying as Prescot, St. Helens and Liverpool that these huge new Norwich first came, and it was not until the year 1887 that they were to be seen in the South of England—much to the consternation of many of the old-established fanciers, who roundly condemned them and declared that they were not Norwich at all!

In the pursuit for size, continual double-buffing was commonly practiced and this, when carried out in excess, led to various undesirable side effects, notably feather tumors, or 'lumps' as they are known to fanciers, which began to spread alarmingly throughout the breed. Even when this evil was not present the production of numerous coarse-feathered, shaggy-thighed birds bore witness to the deterioration in quality that could so easily set in when the critical faculties of fanciers were impaired by blindly following up a new craze.

It was inevitable that a reaction against this trend would eventually set in, and following a good deal of correspondence in the fancy press, a conference was called at the Crystal Palace Show in 1890. At this important gathering, where it was estimated that there were between 300 and 400 breeders present, it was decided that in future the Norwich Plainhead should be judged mainly for type, and the length was to be limited to 6½ inches. The mere fact of passing good resolutions did not of course automatically solve any problems, and many years of painstaking work lay ahead for Norwich fanciers in eradicating the undesirable features that had crept into their breed, while at the same time endeavoring to retain those qualities that had proved advantageous.

Today five different specialist societies cater for the needs of the Norwich canary which, in spite of the turbulent episodes in its past history, remains a breed of great merit and distinction in Great Britain.

DESCRIPTION

'The John Bull of the Canary World' is the favorite cliche of writers when describing the Norwich canary, and this does perhaps convey a general impression of the somewhat rotund and stockily-built figure of the breed as it is today. Although the pursuit of mere size for its own sake has long since been abandoned, it is still a feature of some importance when combined with the primary requirements of type, quality and color, for even though in terms of actual length the Norwich is not the largest breed of canary, it is broadly built and possesses a fair amount of 'body'.

Unlike the Border or the Yorkshire this variety is not required to show any special position or movement, but type is the foremost consideration, for which the greater number of points are allocated on the scale of points for judging. This is not to say however, that carriage of the body is unimportant, for no matter how good its type may be, the appearance of a bird can easily be spoiled by slovenly carriage. The Norwich may not possess the bright and lively manner of the Border nor the stylish elegance of the Yorkshire, but in spite of its stolid and dignified appearance it should move quite freely without any suggestion of sluggishness.

YORKSHIRE CANARY. A self cinnamon "off duty." When it pulls itself together and stands up well it will look a far better bird.

NEW COLOR CANARY. A recessive white.

With reference to type, above all else it should possess a good head which should be large, full and well-rounded, for even though the rest of the body is well proportioned according to standard, a mean-looking head will surely spoil the whole effect. The ideal bird has great width across the top of the skull, without any inclination to flatness or overhanging eyebrows. The beak is short and stout, the cheeks well filled and 'chubby' and the eye clear and bright.

The expression 'bull-necked' is often used to describe the appearance of this particular feature in the ideal Norwich. The neck is short and thick, so short, in fact, as to be almost imperceptible, as the contours of the head merge very quickly into those of the shoulders and chest, and to possess too thin a neck is almost as great a failing as having a mean and narrow skull.

The shortness and stoutness of the neck is repeated in all other features of the body, for the Norwich is the very opposite of being finely drawn and tapered, its whole appearance being broad and well-filled. The body is short and compact but with great depth through from the back to the breast, which is deep and wide and perfectly rounded from throat to tail. The back itself is short and broad, and after rounding the shoulders, almost straight.

The wings and the tail, in common with the other features are short and compact. The wings are carried tightly braced and close to the body, with the tips of the flights just meeting over the rump and the root of the tail. The tail itself is also tightly folded and carried in line with the body, neither being held too high nor dropped too low. The legs are of medium length and well set back, and together with the feet, are strongly made in order to enable the bird to carry itself boldly and confidently well across the perch at an angle of about 40 to 45 degrees.

The features for which the old-fashioned type of Norwich was so highly valued, namely richness of color and quality of feather, still form an important adjunct of the modern version of the breed, although now accounting for a mere 20 per cent of the points allocated instead of over 60 per cent, as in former days. Sufficient has already been said about the importance of good feather quality in respect of other varieties so that little need be added to emphasize the point in a breed that particularly values this characteristic. The feathering of the ideal Norwich is short and compact, soft yet firm and with the highly polished sheen of silk. Any suggestion of looseness or dullness in appearance is completely at variance with the requirements of a perfect exhibition Norwich. The color is as rich and even as possible throughout the whole body of the bird, and in the case of yellow cocks particularly, is a deep golden orange, perhaps almost approaching tangerine in tone.

The usual standard canary colors are to be found throughout the breed, but generally speaking, the white-ground series have been even less popular with Norwich fanciers than with other breeders of type canaries. A small but important section of the fancy consists of the Norwich cinnamons, which at one time were regarded as a separate breed and possessed their own specialist club. Originally these birds were considered first and foremost as cinnamon canaries, which were being bred for exhibition purposes to the Norwich type, but latterly the emphasis was reversed, and correct conformation is now the main consideration with the purity, depth and tone of the cinnamon coloring being subordinate to type. For any fancier who desires to specialize in a strictly limited field this particular section of the fancy should prove most rewarding.

BREEDING

Type, quality and color are constantly recurring words when discussing the breeding of Norwich canaries, for it is mainly on the basis of these points that the fancier must select his pairs. Size, of course, must not be neglected, and on this subject much the same might be said as in the case of the Yorkshire—that for an otherwise perfect bird to be a little short of size is no great detriment, but to allow any deterioration in this direction to go too far is unforgivable in a breed that is essentially strong, well-built and sturdy in character. Size should not be confused with mere length however, for there exist many good, big, heavily-built birds which in fact

RED FACTOR CANARY. A red orange cock. By administering a preparation of canthaxanthin at molting time birds that are very nearly red can be produced.

NORWICH CANARY. The rotund and stocky figure of the breed which has earned for it the nickname of "the John Bull of the canary world."

are somewhat overlong in body and feather for exhibition purposes, although a bird of this description may be useful for mating to a short, compact, high quality partner that may fail a little in size.

Size alone however, is useless, and there is no virtue whatever in breeding from mediocre birds merely because they are big. The first essential must always be type, and although the mating together of two really good, typical show birds does not, of necessity, produce exhibition youngsters, it is only by keeping faithfully to type that an expectation of success on the show bench can eventually be realized.

The ideal Norwich must have a good, large, bold head, and one of the worst defects for breeding in a bird is a head that is too small and mean for the body. Often the skull is too narrow and 'pinched' at the front just above the beak, or it may be too flat on top instead of the desired dome shape. It must have a good, full eyebrow, yet the eye itself should not be obscured by overhanging feather but should always be clear and bold. Yet another fault is that of a large coarse beak, which by comparison tends to make the head look a little smaller.

Birds may occasionally fail by having necks that are rather too long and thin, and some fanciers have recommended that this can be remedied by the simple expedient of a double buff mating. This may well be so, but great care is necessary in selecting the right birds for the purpose otherwise defects in other directions may occur, especially in the matter of feather quality. The beginner is advised once again to keep to orthodox pairings. The hollow neck is often associated with another unpleasant aspect of body shape, namely an arched or 'roach' back which usually results in the wings failing to lie closely on the rump, and it is invariably accompanied by a dropped tail.

The importance of maintaining perfect feather quality must never be neglected in breeding, for even though the framework of the bird is right it will never show to advantage if clothed in poor quality feather. Fortunately if selection is firmly on the basis of short, compact birds the right type of feather will automatically follow, since it is nearly always associated with this kind of bird. It is the over-lengthy ones that generally possess the feathering that is too long, and this is clearly shown by their heavy eyebrows, shaggy thighs and long tail coverts. Good color is also of great importance in one's breeding stock and this must be carefully bred for by selecting birds of good, sound, natural color, for it is quite impossible to get any color into them at molting time if they lack the basic pigments upon which the color food is to act.

It may be found occasionally that Norwich hens are not always the best mothers—which may be said of hens of other breeds as well—but this is rarely so if the big, heavy type of bird is avoided. By nature these are sometimes rather clumsy and inactive, whereas the medium sized, smarter type of hen is as a rule much more lively and energetic in attending to her duties.

MOLTING

The importance of a good molt, and in particular of successful color feeding, should be obvious, for in the Norwich we have the most intensely colored of the leading breeds of canary and it should be the endeavor of every fancier to keep it that way. Although compared with former times color has been relegated to a minor position it is still an essential feature, and a poorly colored bird will stand little chance on the show bench. The very nature of color is to attract the attention, and it is very often just this which first catches the eye of the judge as he approaches a class of exhibits. It is also an obvious truth that, all other points being equal, the better colored bird will always win over a less well colored specimen.

There are several brands of color food on the market, and the beginner may wish to experiment for a while until he finds which give him the best results. More usually however, he is likely to seek the advice and follow the example of an experienced breeder, who is himself a master of the art of color feeding and capable of producing the traditional 'ball of fire' so much admired on the show bench.

BORDER FANCY CANARY. A yellow hen.

EXHIBITING

Compared with the two breeds previously dealt with, training for show is relatively less arduous, but the basic requirements of style and confidence before the judge must be instilled by familiarity with show cage conditions. Lack of steadiness is rarely a fault with the Norwich however, for instead of the sprightly energy displayed by the Border or the swagger of the Yorkshire, they are, if anything, inclined to be placid or even lethargic in the show cage. In spite of their 'comfortable' build it is advisable to train them to move freely from perch to perch displaying some life and energy, for nothing pleases the eye of the judge more than to see a first class Norwich looking the very essence of health and activity.

The standard show cage is of the box-type pattern, being all wood in construction with the exception of the wire front. It has a sloping false roof set at an angle inside the top of the cage which, to allow for convenience in handling, has a small thumb-hole, one inch in diameter, centrally placed.

The cage is 12 inches in width, 11½ inches in height and 5¼ inches in depth, and has a circular door 3½ inches in diameter fitted in the right hand side. The wire front is supported by two strips of wood, the upper one extending ¾ inch from the top of the cage and the lower one 1¾ inches from the base. There is no food trough since it is customary to cover the floor of the cage with plain canary seed when sending out to the shows.

The dimensions of the wire front are 11 inches wide and 8½ inches high, and it consists of 18 wires which, besides the essential bars at top and bottom, have an additional supporting bar 2 inches above the bottom one. The drinker hole is centrally placed on the bottom bar. The front and the outside of the cage are painted black and the interior is finished in a pale shade of bluish-green, known as 'hedge sparrow egg' tint.

The two perches are equally spaced at a convenient distance apart, to allow the bird to move freely from one to the other without its tail touching the sides of the cage when facing inwards. There is no fixed pattern for them but usually about 5/8 inch by ½ inch is a reasonable size for the Norwich canary.

OFFICIAL STANDARD

Some modification to the old standard, decided upon by the Norwich Plainhead Club over eighty years ago, has taken place, and the following is the Standard of Excellence and Scale of Points of the Southern Norwich Plainhead Canary Club, which is agreed to by all specialist societies.

TYPE (25 points): Short and cobby. Back broad and well filled in, showing a slight rise transversely. Chest broad and deep, giving an expansive curved front, and sweeping under therefrom in one full curve to the tail. Ideal length 6 to 6¼ inches. Stance or position at about an angle of 45 degrees.

HEAD (10 points): Proportionately bold and assertive in its carriage. A full forehead rising from a short neat beak. To be well-rounded over and across the skull. Cheeks full and clean-featured, eye to be well placed and unobscured.

NECK (10 points): Short and thick, continuing to run from the back skull on to the shoulders, and from a full throat into the breast.

WINGS (10 points): Short and well braced, meeting nicely at the tips to rest lightly, yet closely, on the rump.

TAIL (5 points): Short, closely packed, and well filled in at the root. Rigidly carried, giving an all-of-one-piece appearance with the body.

LEGS AND FEET (5 points): Well set back. Feet perfect.

CONDITION (10 points): In full bloom of perfect health. Bold and bouncing movement.

QUALITY OF FEATHER (10 points): Close and fine in texture, presenting the smooth, silky plumage necessary to give a clean-cut contour.

COLOR (10 points): Rich, bright and level throughout, with sheen or brilliancy. Yellows a deep orange. Buffs rich in ground color and well mealed.

STAGING (5 points): Clean and correctly staged.

TOTAL — 100 points

14

The Gloster Fancy

HISTORY

Whereas the majority of our canary breeds had their origins in the nineteenth century or earlier, the Gloster Fancy is a creation of the present day and as such is living proof that the modern breeder, no less than his forefathers, has imagination and ability in using the living material he has inherited.

It is to three fanciers in particular that this variety owes its existence; to Mrs. Rogerson of Cheltenham, the original breeder of the miniature crested canaries that were later to bear the name of Gloster Fancy; to J. McLay, a noted Scottish breeder and judge of Crests, who cooperated with Mrs. Rogerson in her breeding program, and to A.W. Smith, the leading canary authority of the present day, without whose enthusiasm and encouragement the new variety might never have gained recognition.

In his book *The Gloster Fancy Canary*, A.W. Smith gives the full story of the first 'Glosters' as they appeared on the showbench at the Crystal Palace in 1925—the only two entries in the novice Crested Canary classes—which he immediately recognized as something entirely new and with an obvious potential for further development. He was instrumental in drawing up the first Standard of Excellence for the new breed, and in christening it the Gloster Fancy in deference to Mrs. Rogerson's native county.

There was of course nothing new about canaries with crests. The mutation first occurred sometime during the eighteenth century, and later appeared in most of the known varieties eventually to achieve popularity as an exhibition form in the Crested Norwich and the Lancashire Coppy.

Both of these breeds however, and also the more modern Crested canary, were very large birds, so that where the Gloster differed completely from its forerunners was in the conception of a miniature canary with a neat little crest instead of the enormous drooping type that had for so long been the ideal of canary fanciers.

On the authority of Mr. Smith it is known that Mrs. Rogerson's original birds were developed by the crossing of crested Rollers with the smallest Borders available, while Mr. McLay's stock consisted of small sized Crests crossed with Borders. Since these two breeders cooperated and exchanged stock it becomes apparent that the Gloster Fancy eventually emerged from a blending of these three sources of blood, the general aim always being to keep the breed small and neat.

This charming little crested variety has so much to recommend it that it was almost inevitable that its success would be assured, although at the outset progress was somewhat slow owing to the indifference and even opposition it encountered from some of the more conservative elements of the fancy. However, in the space of a mere forty years, from 1925 to 1965, it has risen to fourth place in popularity among our canary breeds, and at that time there were already nine specialist clubs in the British Isles to cater for its breeders.

DESCRIPTION

In any crested variety of canary there exist two types of individual, the crested bird itself and its plainheaded counterpart, each of which is an integral part of the breed as a whole. When dealing with some of the simpler aspects of genetics in the canary an explanation of the inheritance of the crested characteristic was given, and it was mentioned that two crested birds are seldom mated together, mainly on account of a lethal factor that is involved. The normal procedure is the mating of crest to plainhead which produces an average of 50 per cent of each type among the progeny, so that any crested variety always consists of approximately equal numbers of crests and plainheads.

This of course is exactly the case with the Gloster Fancy, in which the two types have been given the titles of 'Corona' for the crested form and 'Consort' for the plainhead, and it must be understood that, apart from the difference in head adornment, the bodily conformation of each type is identical, having the same ideal form according to the standard of excellence.

From the outset one of the aims of Gloster breeders has been for a 'tendency towards the diminutive,' so that they have now produced one of the smallest breeds of canary in which show specimens should never exceed 4¾ inches in length. Such small size is not synonymous with meanness however, and the Gloster is a well-built and 'cobby' type of

An experienced exhibitor would gently remove the small white feather from the crest of this corona with a pair of tweezers.

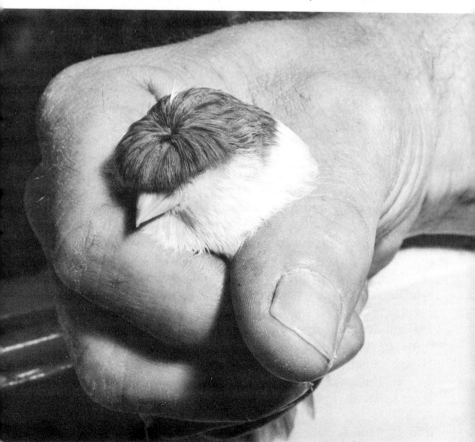

bird in spite of its lack of inches. It would perhaps be over-stressing the case to liken it to a miniature edition of the Norwich, but some of the attributes of the larger breed are looked for to a lesser degree in the smaller one, and the general impression is similar, being that of a short and compact bird without any tendency towards being finely-drawn or racy.

The neck is full and well-filled but without becoming too thick or coarse; the chest is well-rounded in a graceful but not over-prominent curve and the back is fairly broad and again is well-filled. The wings, which should not be too long in the flights, are closely braced to the body and are carried, as required in most breeds, with the tips meeting exactly feather for feather. The tail is fairly short, tightly folded and carried well in line with the general balance of the body.

The legs are of medium length and the bird normally stands at an angle of about 45 degrees. As befits a small canary it is quick and active in its movements, having much the same alert and lively manner as is expected of the Border.

Although the larger breeds of crested canary have a decided tendency to bulkiness and coarseness of feather, in the case of the Gloster the quality of the plumage should be impeccable, being dense and firm, fitting closely to the body, and emphasizing in cleanly cut contours the features so far described. The breed is not color fed but should be of a good natural color whether of yellow or buff.

The crest which is such an important feature of the breed consists of a number of longer feathers on the crown of the head, which radiate evenly all round from a definite center much after the manner of the petals of an old-fashioned double daisy. The center should be clearly discernible but should not disclose anything approaching a 'bald spot' of skin, and the feathers of the crest should lie neatly and in a regular manner all around, with no split or break in the circle and with no roughness or irregularities in the way of 'tufts' or 'horns'. Unlike the older crested varieties the eye remains unobscured, and should be keen and bright.

In the case of the consort the head is bold and well rounded with a decided rise over the center of the skull, much after the manner of the Norwich. It has a good, full eyebrow, yet without the tendency to overhanging feather which would conceal the eye. In keeping with the general appearance of the whole bird the beak also is short and neat, as would be expected, since any coarseness here would at once give an impression of smallness and meanness to the head and crest.

Glosters are to be had in all of the usual standard canary colors, and it may perhaps be worth mentioning that the dominant white has a greater following in this breed than in any other of the popular varieties. Because of the obvious importance of the crest it is the aim of many breeders to produce a dark-crested bird with either a clear body or with even wing marks, and in this particular form a really good Gloster takes on an added attraction.

BREEDING

It has already been made abundantly clear that the correct basic mating is always corona x consort, which may be made either way as may be found desirable. There are however some fanciers who state that they favor the use of corona cocks with consort hens while still others prefer consort cocks and corona hens; but since the crest is produced by a single non-sex-linked gene it is immaterial from which side it is introduced. What is more important is the correct selection of the breeding pairs for all around excellence, and in particular the appreciation of the value of good consorts to mate to the exhibition coronas.

The consort of course carries no gene for the production of a crest as such, but it may well have all the necessary modifying factors governing such items as quality and density of feather, size and width of skull, and so on, which will contribute to the final make-up of its progeny. In short, a good consort that has been bred from a first class exhibition corona can pass on most of the ideal properties it has inherited—with the sole exception of the crest itself.

So important is the selection of an ideal partner for the crested bird that some fanciers have indulged in double consort matings, with a view to the production of good stock consorts for future breeding, but such a procedure is unnecessary, as plenty of good consorts will arise from the normal course of corona x consort matings.

As regards colors the usual rule of yellow to buff *should be applied*, but unfortunately there has been such a widespread use of the double-buff mating in the past that yellow Glosters are in the minority. Breeders now are apt to complain that the reason for their continued use of double-buffing is that there are no good yellows to be obtained, but if this neglect is carried to its logical conclusion ultimately there will be no yellows at all!

The reason for this state of affairs was due to a period of bad judging, during which the larger, bulkier buffs with their bigger crests gained all the recognition, and the smaller, neater yellows, with their shorter feather and smaller crests were overlooked. The lessons of history, in which the craze for double-buffing almost caused the ruination of more than one breed, should be heeded by the Gloster fancier before it is too late, and there is no reason at all why an ideal state should not be arrived at in which yellow and buff are numerically balanced and attain an equal degree of perfection.

In the selection of breeding pairs the guiding principle should be the avoidance, in general terms, of slim, racy birds which always tend to be rather mean-looking, being usually too long in the leg and thin in the neck. Such birds frequently have oval shaped crests instead of the desired circular ones. Although exhibition birds should not exceed 4¾ inches in length, anything slightly oversized need not necessarily be ruled out as good breeding stock, always provided that it has other good properties; but the use of over large birds for their own sake is a mistake, since a 'tendency towards the diminutive' is an important attribute of this breed.

The corona should possess a good center to its crest from which the feathers should radiate in a uniform manner all around. There should be no break whatever in the feather, which should be dense and lie quite flat on the skull. Defects in the conformation of the crest such as tufts, horns, split crests or a bald spot at the back of the skull, are unsightly faults to be avoided if at all possible, but if it is found necessary to use such birds, they may be countered to some extent by the use of consorts that have been well bred from stock that is free from such blemishes.

The Gloster has often been recommended as the ideal beginner's bird and it has sometimes been said of them, a little unkindly perhaps, that they are as easy to breed as mice! It is certainly true that they are very free and prolific, but it must be appreciated that perfection is as difficult to attain in this as in any other variety.

MOLTING

There are no special problems in the molting of Glosters, and not being color fed, the same treatment may be given them as was recommended under the heading of Molting, in the chapter on the Border Fancy. The older, large-crested varieties of canary frequently needed a good deal of assistance at molting time as the feathers of the crest often took some time to break from their quills, but such troubles are rarely encountered in the case of the Gloster.

EXHIBITING

Beyond the normal show cage training which is necessary for all varieties little need be done in the way of general preparation for exhibition. The Gloster is not judged for any attribute such as position, but it is worth noticing that 10 points are allowed on the scale for 'Carriage,' which means in this case a free and lively action, and a further 10 points are allowed for peak condition, health and cleanliness.

The crests of the coronas must always be kept in good condition otherwise little can be expected in the way of prizes in strong competition, and it is often the practice of exhibitors to 'groom' them, using a soft tooth brush which has been made just damp by being dipped in warm water. Even crests that are inclined to be rough or uneven can be much improved by this treatment, as the brushing trains the feather in the direction it should go and furthermore keeps it clean and in good condition. The malpractice of actually 'setting' a crest, using various special preparations, is one that is to be frowned upon.

The show cage is an adaptation suitable for the smaller Gloster Fancy, of the old Crested Canary show cage, being of the box type in which the wire front is curved backwards, or 'bowed' as it is officially described, at the top, thus allowing for an easier inspection of the crest from above. This cage is 12 inches in length, 10 inches in height and 4¾ inches in depth and is painted black externally and eau-de-nil (Nile blue) inside. The wire front which is also painted black must consist of 23 wires with the drinker hole centrally placed, and the drinker itself must also be black.

OFFICIAL STANDARD

The following is the Standard and Scale of Points as issued by the Gloster Fancy Canary Club.

CREST (15 points): Neatness, regular, unbroken round shape, eye discernible.

(5 points): With definite center

CONSORT (15 points): Head broad and round at every point, with good rise over center of skull.

(5 points): Eyebrow heavy, showing brow.

BODY (20 points): Back well filled and wings lying closely thereto; full neck; chest nicely rounded, without prominence.

TAIL (5 points): Closely folded and well carried.

PLUMAGE (15 points): Close, firm, giving a clear-cut appearance; of good natural color.

CARRIAGE.(10 points): Alert, with quick lively movement.

LEGS AND FEET (5 points): Medium length, without blemish.

SIZE (15 points): For tendency to the diminutive.

CONDITION (10 points): Health, cleanliness.

TOTAL — 100 points

15

The Lizard

HISTORY

Among all varieties of the canary the Lizard holds a unique position, for not only is it the oldest breed still in existence but the only one now kept entirely for the pattern and markings of its plumage. It successfully survived the wave of change that overtook most varieties in late Victorian times, as is revealed by an engraving accompanying an article in the *Illustrated London News* of December 12, 1846, which shows it to be the same as the breed of today.

Although this article stated that canary societies had then been in existence for 'upwards of a century,' the actual origin of the Lizard is not known. Traditionally it is accepted that it owed its introduction into this country to the Huguenot refugees, and this belief is given support by a reference in a very old manual which calls it 'the fine *Spangled* Sort commonly called *French Canary Birds*'. Most other breeds bear the name of the locality of their origin but in the case of the Lizard this is not so, and apparently it was named from some resemblance in the pattern of its plumage to the scales of the reptile.

It is in fact almost impossible to designate any particular place as the home of this breed. Originally it was to be found in various centers where the silk weaving industry existed, but eventually it seems to have achieved its main popularity in the North Midlands and Lancashire, where at one time it shared with the very dissimilar Lancashire canary the protection of the specialist society, the Lancashire and Lizard Fanciers Association.

For various reasons the Lizard was never a breed with a large following of admirers and, as a result, it was severely hit by the two world wars of this century: following a careful enquiry, it was estimated that in 1945 there were probably not more than 30 breeding pairs of typical birds left alive. It was realized by a few far-seeing fanciers that if it were once lost this breed could never be re-created, and thus it was that the Lizard Canary Association of Great Britain came to be founded, the primary objective being the saving of this precious remnant from extinction.

To ensure the continuance of the breed, and to prevent its dissipation among experimental breeders or possible exploitation by speculators, a strong policy to safeguard this nucleus stock of Lizard canaries was necessary, and so successful were the efforts of the L.C.A. that today the breed is thriving once more. Although possibly never destined for the widespread popularity of the major breeds of canary this splendid old variety will always prove attractive to the connoisseur, both on account of its historical interest and its unique characteristics.

DESCRIPTION

Unlike the main breeds of canary which are the result of selective breeding in various directions, the Lizard is a distinct mutation which, as recent experimental work has shown, behaves as a recessive to the normal wild-type, self green canary.

Variegation is not a characteristic and there is no counterpart in the Lizard to the clear, ticked, marked and variegated birds of other varieties. All birds are dark-plumaged selfs, possessing the same basic pigments as the wild green canary and, save for the 'cap,' which is an area of clear feathers on the crown of the head, no light feathering should be found on any part of the body. In the cap however some variation can and does occur, and this is used to form a basis for the classification of the breed.

As with all varieties of canary there are two basic colors to be found, but in the Lizard the ancient terminology is still employed and the two main color divisions are known as 'gold' and 'silver,' which correspond to the terms 'yellow' and 'buff' as used in other sections of the canary fancy. In the gold birds the dark ground color of the feather is edged with a deep golden-yellow whereas in the silvers it is terminated by a fine margin of white, similar to the frosting of a buff canary.

Although the distinctive cap is often the first thing to catch the eye it is not the most important characteristic of the breed, this being reserved for the feature which really makes the Lizard what it is, namely the spangling. Briefly, this is a series of black, crescent-shaped spots running in orderly parallel rows down the back of the bird, produced by the overlapping of the saddle feathers. Each of these has a ground color of deep bronze which merges into a black zone towards the center of the web. This zone broadens out as it approaches the outer margin of the feather but stops just short of the edge, which is then terminated by the narrow fringe of gold or silver as the case may be. Such feathers when in their natural overlapping position on the bird give rise to the typical pattern of crescent-shaped spangles.

Owing to the peculiar nature of the Lizard mutation this description of the spangling applies only to bird in their full show plumage. It is not applicable to the young birds in their nest feather, at which stage they are not unlike ordinary young green canaries. With each successive molt the marginal fringe of color increases in width, until eventually the spangling becomes clouded and indistinct.

Markings of a similar nature to the spangling are also reproduced on the breast, but owing to the slight difference in shape and texture between breast and saddle feathers, they are rarely so sharply defined. These markings are technically known as 'rowings,' and in the ideal bird they too are in perfect lines, extending from throat to tail and across the breast from both sides well towards the center. The covert feathers also possess the distinct lacing of lighter color around the edges.

As in any self canary, the wings and tail of the Lizard consist of entirely dark feathers, and it is considered a grave fault for a bird to be 'foul-tailed' or 'foul-winged'. Ideally, the quill feathers should be as near to jet black as possible, and this applies also to the beak, legs, feet and claws.

This photograph shows something of the spangling of the Lizard canary although this bird lacks a good deal of marking on the shoulder. It also has the fault of a cap that has a tendency to "run" at the back.

It was mentioned earlier that the basic color of the Lizard is that of a green canary, but this must only be taken to mean that it is a yellow ground bird with the dark pigments of black and brown, superimposed as described in an earlier chapter. Actually any suggestion of a true greenish shade is unwelcome, and by selective breeding has largely been eliminated so that the ground color of the Lizard is really much nearer to bronze. Since color feeding is customary in this variety, the effect ultimately produced is that of a deep chestnut in the golds and a warm bronze-grey in the silvers.

The cap of the Lizard is certainly a most distinctive feature and is usually the one most remarked upon by the non-fancying public. In the ideal bird it covers the crown of the head and roughly follows the line of the skull, being oval in shape and extending from the base of the upper mandible to the back of the head. It should have a clearly defined edge and pass just above the eye, from which it is separated by a thin line of dark feathers known as the 'eyelash'. At one time in the past only this perfect form of clear cap was countenanced in a show Lizard, but nowadays classes are provided for broken-caps and non-caps as well.

Excellent feather quality is obviously an essential in this breed, for how else could the complicated pattern of markings be clearly displayed? Any suggestion of coarseness or of looseness would destroy the illusion at once, so that it is true to say that any poor feather quality has long since been eliminated from the variety.

It will be noted that no mention has been made of any particular type of Lizard canary, and in fact it is not basically a bird of type or position. It is however, somewhat reminiscent of the Border Fancy in general shape and style, but is a shade smaller being only 4¾ to 5 inches in length. It is an extremely active bird with an abundance of nervous energy, and although not numerically among the leaders in the canary world is undoubtedly one of the most highly esteemed—and of course it is irreplaceable.

BREEDING

The correct method for mating in Lizard canaries is gold to silver, and any temptation to indulge in double gold or double silver breeding must be as firmly avoided as in the case of double yellowing or double buffing in other breeds. In the matter of caps it is customary to pair a clear-cap to a broken- or non-capped bird, but broken-cap to broken-cap is also a useful mating, and from these a fair selection of the different forms of cap can be expected. The mating together of clear-capped birds however, is seldom advisable as it very often leads to the production of birds with overlarge caps.

Every breed has its own particular failings and these must be carefully avoided when selecting breeding pairs, in order to prevent them from being perpetuated. In the case of the Lizard the faults that arise are mainly in the nature of mismarkings of various descriptions, the most objectionable of which is the 'bald-face'. In this, the light feathering of the cap encroaches to a varying degree upon the face and cheeks or under the beak, and is regarded such a grave blemish that it entails automatic disqualification from competition. Scarcely less serious is the 'over-capped' bird, in which the cap continues too far down the neck. Birds with such faults should not be used for breeding but can be disposed of as songsters.

The presence of light feathering anywhere but in the cap has already been mentioned as contrary to the conception of a perfect Lizard, so that any birds with white feathers in the wings or tail or among the coverts must also be banned from the breeding cage. Equally objectionable are greyish or grizzled feathers instead of sound, dark ones, for they are usually indicative of a bird that is running too light in ground color. This also often manifests itself in light, flesh-colored beak, legs and feet.

The ideal bird for breeding should have a deep, even ground color, free from any tinge of green or suggestion of dullness or smokiness, sound dark wings and tail and fine and satiny feather quality. Its distinctive markings—the spangling on the back and the rowings on the breast—should be dense and profuse, and should be clearly defined so as to contrast sharply with the ground color.

Lizards are not particularly difficult birds to breed and may be subjected to any of the standard systems of management. The only point upon which the breeder needs to exercise any special vigilance is to ensure that there is no damage to the plumage in the way of feather plucking, since this may seriously affect a bird's chances on the showbench.

MOLTING

No breed requires greater care and attention at molting time, since it is entirely upon its plumage that the bird is judged. The effect of the mutation which gave rise to the Lizard was to induce a gradual disappearance of the melanin pigments from the extreme distal edge of each feather at successive molts, and this explains why the young bird in nestling plumage has no spangling—it is only when the body feathers are replaced at the first molt that the typical pattern is produced. At this stage the wing and tail feathers are not normally shed, thus remaining entirely dark, and it is this combination of once-shed body feathers and unflighted wing and tail feathers that give rise to the perfect show bird.

It will readily be appreciated that if any feather is shed other than at its proper time it will be replaced by another which is one stage ahead in the cycle of development. In the case of the flight and tail feathers this will be particularly noticeable, since the disappearance of the dark melanin pigment will leave an area of *white* at the tip. Every possible precaution should therefore be taken to avoid the unnatural casting of these feathers, and this can best be done by molting the birds singly in order to prevent any damage by plucking or fighting.

All this may tend to make the Lizard sound a difficult breed to deal with, but such is not actually the case, for although the premature loss of wing or tail feathers must be avoided if at all possible, it is not the end of the road for a bird if such a mishap should occur. No disqualification from the showbench is involved, although it must be realized that the blemish will count against the bird to some extent.

EXHIBITING

Not being judged for type or position the Lizard does not require any extensive training for show, but it must be absolutely steady when the cage is handled and should hop obediently from one perch to the other, so that the judge can examine it carefully on both sides. Any tendency to wildness will usually result in the plumage becoming disarranged and the regular order of the markings being disturbed.

The standard show cage is of the box type with a wire front, but with a sloping top instead of the more usual flat one. The height at the front is 12 inches and at the back 9¾ inches. The length also is 12 inches and the depth from front to back 4½ inches, the wood for construction being 3/16 inch thick. These are all outside measurements.

The cage is fitted with a circular door on the right hand side which is 3½ inches in diameter and is hinged at the top, the lowest point of the door being 3 inches from the floor. On the same side and just inside the cage is a feeding trough, fitted on the floor, which is 1½ inches from the side and 1 inch deep.

The strips of wood which support the wire front extend 1 inch from the top of the cage and 1¾ inches from the bottom. The front itself is made from four strips of punched bar with 9 inches between the top and bottom ones, and two supporting ones being 1½ inches from top and bottom respectively. They are 11½ inches in length and have 18 wires which are 5/8 inch apart center to center. The drinker hole is in the center at the bottom of the wire front. The cage is finished in black enamel on the outside and a pale shade of blue, known as 'Nursery Blue,' on the inside.

The perches are not standardized and the exhibitor may use any pattern of his choice; the same is true of the floor covering, although it is fairly widespread practice to utilize a thick piece of white blotting paper cut to size, which has already been recommended on account of its absorbent qualities. The drinkers may be of metal or plastic but should be enamelled black on the outside.

OFFICIAL STANDARD

The Lizard Canary Association issues a very detailed description of the ideal bird, prefacing it with a note that 'Golds and Silvers, Capped or Non-capped, Cocks or Hens, may all attain an equal standard' and that 'Broken-capped birds which are equal to the ideal in all respects other than the cap will only lose a proportion of the ten points for the cap according to the extent of the blemish'.

The description, which is of a clear-capped gold cock, is as follows:

The bird is 4¾ inches in length, neither over-stout nor too slim. It stands quietly and confidently on the perch at an angle of 45 degrees. The ground color is uniform in depth and is a rich golden bronze entirely free from any suggestion of other shade. The spangling is clear and distinct, each individual spangle being clear of another. It extends from the edge of the cap in perfectly straight lines to the wing coverts, each successive spangle being progressively larger than the one nearer the neck.

The feather quality is of conspicuous silkiness, the feathers being close and tight with no suggestion of coarseness or looseness.

The breast is round and fairly full without giving any impression of stoutness. The rowings are clear and distinct from one another and are lineable. They extend from near the eye down to the base of the tail and across the breast from both sides well towards the center.

The wing feathers are compact and held closely to the body. Their tips meet in a straight line down the center of the back. They are so dark, except at the extreme edges, as to appear almost black.

The tail is narrow, straight and neat with feathers of the quality and color of the wing feathers.

The head is fairly large, round and full on the top. The cap extends from the beak to the base of the skull and is oval in shape with a clearly defined edge. It is clear of the eye, being separated therefrom by the eyelash which is a well-defined line of dark feathers extending to the base of the upper mandible. There are no dark feathers between the cap and the upper mandible. The cap is a deep golden orange color and has no blemishes of dark or light feather.

The covert feathers are clear, distinct and lineable and so dark as to appear almost black. They are distinctly laced round the edges.

The beak, legs and feet are dark.

The bird is in perfect condition, quite steady and staged correctly.

SCALE OF POINTS

SPANGLES (25 points): For regularity and distinctness.
FEATHER QUALITY (15 points): For tightness and silkiness.
GROUND COLOR (10 points): For depth and evenness.

BREAST (10 points): For extent and regularity of rowings.
WINGS AND TAIL (10 points): For neatness and darkness.
CAP (10 points): For neatness and shape.
COVERT FEATHERS (5 points): For darkness and lacing.
EYELASH (5 points): For regularity and clarity.
BEAK, LEGS AND FEET (5 points): For darkness.
STEADINESS AND STAGING (5 points)

TOTAL — 100 points

Condition is taken for granted. Any bird which, in the opinion of the judge, is not in perfect health or which shows any physical defect shall not be credited with any points for other virtues.

In classes for non-capped Lizards points to a maximum of ten are awarded for the perfection of the spangling on the head.

16

Other Varieties of British Origin

One of the many interesting aspects of the canary fancy concerns the fluctuation in popularity of the various breeds at different periods of their history. Why it should be that certain varieties have gained widespread recognition while others have remained relatively neglected is a complex question, and still more so is the case of those that were once flourishing and yet have become exceedingly rare, or even extinct, within a comparatively short space of time.

Changes in taste on the part of fanciers, the availability and price of stock, and above all, ease in breeding, are some of the main factors contributing to these changes of status, and it is also probably true to say that during the past few decades the great majority of fanciers have had neither the patience nor the inclination to persevere with the more difficult 'fancy' varieties that were once popular in Victorian times.

It is a matter of great regret that several of these interesting types have now gone beyond the point of any possible redemption and exist only in a degenerate state, for they often represented the very pinnacle of the breeder's art and one which, judging by present-day trends, the modern fanciers would seem to have little chance of emulating. A whole field of work is open to the enthusiast who might be interested in reviving the fortunes of those varieties that have not yet gone too far, and if he were able to help in ensuring the continuance of some of the older breeds he would be rendering a valuable service to the entire fancy.

THE CRESTED CANARY

To the old-time fancier it would be unthinkable that such a wonderful example of the breeder's art as the Crested canary should ever have to be relegated to a chapter on 'other varieties'. At one time it had a tremendous following, and besides being the subject of intense competition at the shows it commanded some of the highest prices ever paid for birds in the canary fancy. Today, unfortunately, it is in the hands of very few breeders, so that numerically at least, it must be regarded as a minor variety.

The Crested canary is a breed of ancient lineage which at one time rejoiced in the old-fashioned title of 'Turn-crown' or 'Turncrest,' but when the mutation first occurred is not known. No mention of Crested canaries was made in any of the earlier editions of Hervieux, but Dr. Galloway records that he found it included in the 1793 London edition of Buffon's *Natural History*, as an addition to Hervieux' 1713 list, and thus it can be inferred that it was first encountered sometime between these two dates. The crested characteristic probably pre-dated the development of most individual breeds, for by mid-Victorian times it was to be found in several varieties including the Norwich, Lancashire and Belgian, as well as among common canaries and German Rollers.

The canary breeders of Norwich appear to have been the first to recognize the show potential of the crested bird. They eventually incorporated it with their own local breed, so that by the middle of the century there existed side by side the Norwich Plainhead and the Crested Norwich, which old illustrations show to be almost identical, with the presence or absence of the crest as the only distinguishing feature. Unfortunately the Norwich ideals of that time, consisting as they did of rich coloring and superb feather quality, imposed severe limitations upon the breeders of the crested bird, for it was a near impossibility to have long and profuse feathering of the crest coupled with fine and close body feather. The crests of those day, although perfect in their way, were small by comparison with the modern bird, and in an effort to increase their size breeders looked to the Lancashire canary.

This was an immense bird, almost eight inches in length, coarse in feather but with a large crest falling well over the beak and eyes, so that the results of the outcross brought about a radical alteration to the Crested Norwich, producing a larger, coarser type of bird but with a vastly improved crest.

The first examples of this outcross are known to have been exhibited in 1879, but were rejected by the judges on that occasion who recognized them for what they were. The seeds of the idea had been sown however, and it was not long before many more birds of this type were on the show benches and commanding the attention of the fancy. Even as late as 1911, Claude St. John stated that fanciers were still crossing Coppies with their Crested stock, although by then most of the pioneer work had been done and a vast amount of improvement towards a new ideal had taken place.

The new Crested canaries became a sensational craze among fanciers, and eventually reached a peak of popularity which caused them to claim for their birds the title of 'King of the Fancy,' which had once been borne by the Belgian. Fantastic prices were paid for outstanding specimens, and C.A. House, writing in 1923 stated that the Crest fancy had become entirely a rich man's hobby, adding that by then Crest breeders were not one in fifty compared with the numbers twenty-five to thirty years earlier.

Prohibitive prices were not the only reason for the decline of the Crested canary. In their efforts to produce even bigger and better crests, continual double-buffing was practiced by the breeders until, after several generations, the disfiguring side effects of blindness and 'lumps' became so widespread that many fanciers gave up in despair. Although these troubles are less prevalent today, numerically, the position of the breed has failed to improve. A few specimens are to be seen at some of the larger shows in the country, serving as living examples of some of the achievements of breeders of the past.

The Crested canary of today possibly shows some reduction in size when compared with the breed in its heyday, but it is still a largish bird with a profusion of feathering on head and body. As with all crested varieties, two types of individual exist to make up the breed as a whole, and in this case the crested bird is known simply as the 'Crest' and the plain-headed form as the 'Crest-bred'. Apart from the obvious differences in their head properties, the ideals regarding the general body characteristics are the same in each case.

The breed possesses a massive head, a short, thick neck and a broad, deep body which, according to the Crested Canary Club, should somewhat resemble that of the bull-finch in shape. The bird stands fairly low across the perch on shortish legs which are well set back, and the wings and tail are closely folded and should not be too long.

However, it is to the crest that by far the greatest importance is attached, and many judges of the past looked at nothing else! The crest can never be too large and round, the standard object of comparison in the old days being a five shilling (fifty-cent) piece, and it consists of an abundance of broad, long feathers radiating evenly from a small center well over the eyes, beak and back of the head. A flat crest is tolerated only if it is well filled and free from other defects, and preference is always given to the heavy drooping type that fanciers usually refer to as a 'weeping' crest. The various faults that were described in the case of the Gloster Fancy, such as splits, tufts, horns, or anything other than a perfectly circular crest, are equally objectionable in this variety and should never be bred from if it is at all avoidable.

The head of the crest-bred should be large and rounded, broad at every point and with a small, neat beak. There should be an abundance of long, broad feathers continuing over the crown of the head which, if turned back with a pencil, should reach the tip of the beak. The head should also possess heavy eyebrows which, just as effectively as in the crested bird, hide the eyes from view and give the crest-bred something of a frowning or sulky appearance.

Although Crested canary breeders endeavor to keep the body as neat and compact as possible, good feather quality is not a notable feature of the breed. Many of the best specimens look decidedly rough and shaggy, but this is only to be expected when the main aim is breeding for length of feather

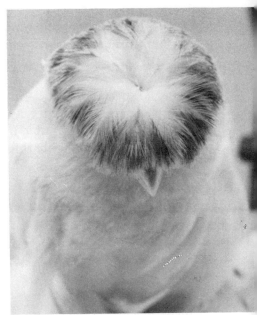

The Crest Mutation. This plain-headed bird, known as crest-bred, is the correct partner for a crest. Their progeny will consist of approximately equal numbers of each.

The Crest Mutation. The ideal well-radiated circular crest is seen here although this bird lacks a little in "frontal" which should come well over the end of the beak.

on the head, since this cannot be achieved without producing it on the body as well. So far as color is concerned this is of no special importance, and like the Gloster, yellows are in the minority due to the prevalence of double-buffing for so many years. Clear-bodied, dark-crested birds are most attractive in appearance, as are the dark-crested, wing-marked individuals, and it is every breeder's aim to produce a winning specimen of this description. Markings in themselves, however have no preference on the show bench, and a heavily variegated or green bird of better type would win over a perfectly marked but inferior type of bird.

The breeding of these large Crested canaries necessitates various small modifications to the usual routine of canary keeping, among which may be mentioned the provision of larger drinker holes to prevent any damage to the crests; the setting of the perches in a lower position in the cages owing to the restricted upwards vision of the birds, and the trimming of the crest away from the beak and above the eyes, as a preliminary to the breeding season. Apart from this however, no special difficulties need be expected, for if healthy, Crests are quite free breeders and normally rear their own young without any trouble and without the aid of 'feeders'.

It is regrettable that this striking variety, with its interesting historical background, should be condemned to linger on in such small numbers as to make its continued existence precarious. There will probably always be a few fanciers however, to whom the challenge of breeding a bird with such highly developed characteristics will make an appeal, and to them must be entrusted the future of this grand old breed.

THE FIFE FANCY

In contrast to the poultry fancy, where bantams are generally more popular than the larger fowl, in the canary world the concept of miniature editions of the standard breeds has never aroused any great enthusiasm, and classes that have been provided for their encouragement have, in general, received negligible support. The most recent addition to the list of canary varieties however, which has been christened the Fife Fancy, is in effect a miniature Border Fancy, but whether it will ever receive any wide-spread attention is a matter of conjecture.

The Fife Fancy Canary Club was formed at a meeting held in 1957 at Kirkaldy in Fifeshire, Scotland, its main object being to sponsor the breeding and exhibiting of these miniatures, and it is perhaps of some significance that the foundation of this society should have coincided with a period of some dissatisfaction at the trend in normal Borders towards an increase in size. At all events, it has provided an opportunity for those fanciers who wish to keep their "wee gems" really small, and enables them to continue to exhibit their birds without being handicapped in the matter of size.

The pictorial model and the wording of the official standard is almost identical to that of the Border Fancy, but some adjustment has been made to the number of points awarded to the various features in order to allow a total of 20 to be given for smallness of size which, it is stated, *should not exceed* 4¼ *inches.* The show cage for Fifes is also based upon that of the Border, but it has some minor differences including a somewhat smaller size, in keeping with the character of the breed.

THE LANCASHIRE

It was something of a tragedy for the whole canary fancy when the Lancashire canary became extinct during the second World War. The loss is the greater when the unique character of the bird is considered, for not only was it one of the crested varieties but also among the largest of breeds.

Like the Belgian, it was called upon to contribute too much of its life blood to other breeds and probably no other breed was destined to play such an important part in the evolution of new types; but unfortunately it found relatively few admirers for its own sake outside the boundaries of its native county, and thus remained essentially a local breed. Even before the first World War, Claude St. John (*Our Canaries*, 1911) foresaw the inherent danger to the breed of this extreme localization, and commented that 'although it is still a great favorite in its home county and in not the slightest danger of extinction, *this is no criterion for its future popularity*,' and regrettably this has proved only too true.

Like all crested breeds the Lancashire existed in the two forms, and for these the terms 'Coppy' and 'Plainhead' were always applied, corresponding to 'Crest' and 'Crest-bred,' or 'Corona' and 'Consort' in the breeds that have already been dealt with. Unlike either of these however, whose crests are more or less circular in form, the coppy of the Lancashire was of a horseshoe shape, flowing forward and outward over the beak and eyes with perfect radiation. At the back of the head the feathers lay well down, with no suggestion of roughness, and merged imperceptibly with the feathers at the back of the neck. In the plain-headed bird the abundance of long feather on the head gave rise to overhanging eyebrows, much as in the modern crest-bred, giving it a stolid, almost sulky appearance.

In bodily conformation the Lancashire was massively built throughout, though not over-stout. The body was long and tapering and well filled, with wide shoulders, a broad straight back and a full breast. The neck was of fair length but full and thick, in keeping with the heavy build of the variety. Wings and tail were long and compact; legs strong and straight, and the attitude of the bird was nearly erect, giving it a bold and commanding appearance. Feather quality was not notably good, but this was only to be expected in so large a breed where 25 points were awarded for the coppy alone, and 20 points for size.

In color, the Lancashire existed in the usual yellow and buff of all canaries, but it is worthy of remark that variegated plumage was unknown in this breed. All birds were clears, and the only departure from this ideal that was tolerated was in the case of a ticked or grey coppy. Breeding procedure was the same as in other crested varieties, but the Lancashire was inclined to be somewhat lethargic in performing its parental duties so that fanciers often kept feeding pairs as foster parents.

As has already been explained in the relevant chapters, this breed was extensively used during the latter years of the nineteenth century to cross with the Crested Norwich and the Norwich Plainhead, thus laying the foundations of the modern Crested canary and the modern Norwich. The Yorkshire too was created with the help of a large percentage of Lancashire blood. Bearing these facts in mind, it will be apparent that it should not be an impossible task (albeit a somewhat lengthy one) to recreate the breed. The genetic material is still there, waiting to be reassembled, among the varieties to which the Lancashire contributed in the past. Members of the Old Varieties Canary Association of Great Britain, founded in 1970 to preserve the old and rare breeds from extinction, have already applied themselves to this task and some very useful stock is now emerging.

THE LONDON FANCY
No treatise on canaries can be considered as complete without some reference being made to that beautiful but

long-extinct variety, the London Fancy, for possibly no other has been more talked about or less understood. As a living and flourishing breed it belonged to the very early days of organized fancying, and even the veteran fanciers of today have probably never seen a genuine, pure-blooded London Fancy. A few degenerate examples have existed in the present century, but these were so swamped with alien blood that they scarcely merited the title, and claims that have been made from time to time that the breed has been revived have never stood up to investigation.

According to the *Illustrated London News* of December 12, 1846, this was an important exhibition variety at that time, and had been for many years past, so it is perhaps difficult to appreciate that by the later years of the century it was verging on extinction. The fact is however, that like the Lancashire, the London Fancy was a very local specialty, almost entirely confined to the London area, and specimens were never very numerous. The article in the periodical referred to mentions that there were four different societies of fanciers in London devoted to this canary, and yet the Rev. Francis Smith (*The Canary, its Varieties, Management and Breeding*, 1868) tells of the difficulties he had in obtaining a pair of London Fancies for his collection.

Further evidence of diminishing numbers came from a prominent breeder writing to W.A. Blakston in 1878. Deploring the low state to which the breed had declined, he wrote, 'I doubt whether there are at the present time a hundred London Fancy canaries in existence'.

In the year 1894, by which time the older societies were no longer functioning, an attempt to rally interest in the variety was made with the formation of the London Fancy Club; but evidently things had already gone too far, for even in its best year (1897), a total of only 33 specimens were exhibited. Long before this however, in an effort to save the breed, fanciers had been resorting to outcrosses with other varieties but this, if anything, actually hastened the end, since the process caused most of the special characteristics of the breed to be lost.

Contemporary illustrations and descriptions reveal the London Fancy in its show plumage to have been of a beautiful golden yellow color, with dark wings and tail. Many fanciers have thus assumed that it was a kind of variegated bird, similar to an evenly marked specimen of one of the present-day varieties, in which, by skillful selection, the clear areas had been confined to the body and the dark areas to the wings and tail. A careful reading of all the available literature on the breed however, will reveal that this was not so, and that it was basically a dark self variety which underwent an unusual plumage change at molting time, in a similar manner to its close relative the Lizard.

In juvenile plumage in fact, the Lizard and the London Fancy were almost identical, and the difference between the two could scarcely be distinguished even by the most experienced fanciers. The body feathers in this phase were greenish-brónze with dark pencilling, in the usual manner of the common green or wild-type canary, the wings and tail of course also being dark. At the adult molt both breeds assumed their most perfect exhibition form, the nest feather plumage of the Lizard being replaced by the spangled pattern, with the light colored edging to the feathers, and that of the London Fancy by feathers which became light colored all over the web and not only at the edges as in the Lizard.

It is also known that at one time during the early years of the breed intermediate types, called 'spangle-backs,' were quite common, which to a greater or lesser extent retained some dark marking, or in which the melanins remained as faintly grey or grizzled ticks. The wing and tail feathers, not being shed at the first molt, remained dark and unaltered so that the perfect one year show bird was produced. It is evident that these differences were due merely to a differing degree of expression of the same mutant gene which, as explained in the chaper on the Lizard, causes the disappearance of melanin pigment from certain areas of the feather.

Most of the old writers, who of course had never even heard of Mendel, stated as a simple matter of fact that if crossed with other varieties the characteristic markings disappeared, which points to the fact that this was a recessive mutation, and experimental work with the Lizard confirms this view. It becomes obvious therefore how out-crosses to clear or variegated birds of other breeds caused the final extinction of the London Fancy. The plumage pattern being a recessive would disappear at the first cross, but the old fanciers, although not possessing any genetical knowledge, would at least know from practical experience that a back-cross would next be needed. From this mating however, owing to the variegation factors which would by now have become involved, it would have been practically impossible to tell which birds were 'pure' for the London Fancy factor, and which were merely carriers. These variegated crossbred London Fancies were typical of the few degenerate specimens which lingered on into the present century, some preserved skins of which can be examined in the Natural History Museum in London. In the hands of badly informed fanciers a recessive mutation can be very easily lost, and this, sadly, is what happened to the beautiful and historically interesting London Fancy canary.

THE SCOTCH FANCY

To any admirer of the more unusual breeds of canary the decline of the Scotch Fancy to a perilously low position must be regarded with more than a little concern, for although once popular in its native land, it is now a rarity. The seriousness of the situation is clearly revealed if a comparison is made between entries at shows in the time of Blakston with those of the present day. Writing in 1878, this authority mentions visiting exhibitions in Glasgow where anything up to 1,000 of these birds could be seen, but at the leading shows today it is rare for more than a dozen or so specimens to be on view.

The origin of so unusually shaped a bird as the Scotch Fancy may give rise to some speculation, but Blakston was in no doubt about the matter, firmly believing that it was a development from imported Belgian stock dating back at least to the 1830's. During the middle years of the century the breed had achieved considerable popularity among Scottish fanciers, particularly among the more populous Central Lowlands, and during that period it became known by the local name of 'Glasgow Don'.

Like so many other canaries the Scotch Fancy underwent a considerable change of type in late Victorian times, so much so that a glance at illustrations of the old and new styles of bird would scarcely suggest that they were of the same breed. These changes were brought about as a result of the re-introduction of Belgian blood, which was carried out so consistently that eventually it was almost impossible to tell the two breeds apart, and apparently, according to St. John, it was quite possible, and frequently happened, for a bird to be exhibited with equal success as either variety. 'The blending of these two breeds has been fraught with evil results to the general welfare of both,' he wrote, (*Our Canaries*, 1911), 'and has undoubtedly contributed in no small measure in various ways to the decline of both breeds in popularity.'

This need not have been so, for although there certainly is a marked general resemblance between the two, certain outstanding features make them easily distinguishable and it is only in the case of inferior examples that confusion might arise. The straight back and stiffly braced legs of the Belgian give way in the Scotch Fancy to a markedly *curved* back, with the tail sweeping well under the perch, and much more supple legs. In show position too, the head of the Scotch Fancy is thrust more forward and has a less pronounced droop, while the shoulders, although still prominent, have not the width and massive build of those of the Belgian.

Here again is one of the old-time 'birds of position,' with a special type of posture to show off its points to full advantage. But in addition to the usual general attributes of type and position must be added a third one—action, for it is an essential characteristic of the Scotch Fancy to be a free mover, full of jaunty bearing and confident carriage. In position it is erect upon the perch, the head carried well forward with the neck extended, and forming with the back and tail a continuous graceful curve. The throat, breast and under surface of the body also form one harmonious curve, which in the finest specimens gives the impression of having been hollowed out on a lathe. Feather quality not being notably good however, this line is often spoiled by a certain amount of fluffiness.

YORKSHIRE CANARY. A clear buff, standing "at ease."

The action, or 'traveling' as it is known, is an integral part of the exhibition of the Scotch Fancy, and at one time was considered so important that 25 points out of 100 were allocated for the performance. The show cage is of a pattern similar to, though somewhat larger than, the present-day Border Fancy cage, and in its action the bird should travel smartly from perch to perch in a sprightly and active manner, with no sign of sluggishness nor of nervousness. It should hop from one perch to the opposite one and immediately face about, falling naturally into its characteristic position, and it should continue to do this as often as is required by the judge. It should never use its wings for assistance, nor hesitate in any way, nor steady itself by gripping the wires with its foot or by pressing its tail against the perch. Freedom of movement, liveliness of action, and the sharp way in which it turns itself round into position are the essentials of the performance.

Regrettably few of the Scotch Fancies of today are trained to this pitch of perfection, but there are some fanciers at least who still care for this fascinating variety, and hope to restore to it something of its former glory. This is another field in which members of the Old Varieties Canary Association are interesting themselves and are 'breeding back' to the old type of bird that was popular in late Victorian times. As yet however, stocks are still low, and until a reasonable supply of moderately priced birds is available there is small hope of it becoming re-established in popular favor.

17

Varieties from Continental Europe

Although the fanciers from Europe have, in the main, made the Roller their specialty, various type breeds have also been developed in certain countries. Few peoples however, except the Flemish, seem to have had quite the same success in this direction as the English fancier so that continental type breeds are fewer in number and in variety than those dealt with in the preceding chapters.

As was mentioned earlier it was particularly from people like the Flemings that the idea of 'fancying' seems to have developed and very many famous breeds of livestock, such as the Flemish giant rabbit, the Antwerp pigeon and the Barbu d'Anvers bantam, come from this area. It also seems likely that many of the European breeds of canary, and indeed some of the English ones, emanated from an ancestral type bred in the Low Countries during the eighteenth century, and often referred to by writers as the 'Old Dutch' canary. It was evidently the progenitor of the Belgian, the Scotch Fancy, all of the frilled breeds and probably even the Lancashire so that it must be regarded as a very important basic source of material.

THE BELGIAN

Pride of place among all of the old canaries must go to the Belgian, not only on account of the esteem in which it was held by connoisseurs of the fancy, but also on account of its influence on the breeding of other varieties. In the middle

PAIR OF GLOSTER FANCY CANARIES. A standard mating, consisting of a corona (crest) and a consort (plainhead), which produces fifty percent of each type among the progeny.

YORKSHIRE CANARY. A blue variegated white with eye and wing markings.

of the nineteenth century it was accorded by fanciers the title of 'king' of the canary world and exceptionally high prices were regularly paid for outstanding show birds.

As a breed it ranks among the very oldest, and canary societies are known to have existed in Belgium in the early part of the nineteenth century. Its long 'reign' extended throughout the century and it was freely exported from Belgium to other centers of canary culture where it was appreciated either for its own sake or as a valuable source of material for the improvement of native varieties, such as the Yorkshire and Scotch Fancy in Britain.

By the turn of the century, however, the Belgian was already beginning to lose ground and the leading authorities of the day attributed this almost entirely to the inroads that were being made into Belgian stocks for the purpose of improving other breeds. Although this was to some extent offset by the continued dedication and single-mindedness of many Belgian breeders, the coming of the first World War ensured the near extinction of the breed in its original homeland—a blow from which it has never really recovered. Efforts by some enthusiasts to preserve what remained of the decimated stocks, coupled with the use of breeds to which it contributed in the past, resulted in the Belgian becoming re-established during the 1920's and 30's. The second World War however dealt another severe blow and the whole work had to be repeated with very little true material now available so that the present-day Belgian is a somewhat degenerate example of the breed as it was in its heyday.

Upon seeing illustrations of Belgian canaries for the first time most people at once remark upon their peculiar appearance and even imagine that they may be deformed, until it is explained that this breed is the foremost of all the 'birds of position' and can take up its striking stance in the show cage whenever required to do so, in much the same way as certain varieties of fancy pigeon. The main essentials of a high class Belgian are epitomized in the two words *shape* and *position* and little else is of any consequence. In its better days it was a largish bird, often running well over seven inches in length, but the modern Belgian is generally no larger than a Roller.

In comparison with many other breeds the head is small in proportion to the body and is neat, finely modeled and somewhat flattish on the crown, giving it what fanciers term a 'snaky' appearance. The same epithet is applied to the neck which is long and slender and capable of being much extended. The body is long and tapered, with a straight back and closely braced wings; but the great feature which distinguishes the Belgian from all other canaries is its high prominent shoulders which give it the remarkable hump-backed appearance so characteristic of the breed and embodied in its native name of *Belgische Bult* or *Bossu Belge*.

The bird also has very long legs which often tend to show quite a length of thigh joint, and they are held straight and stiff with little flexibility at the 'elbow'. This peculiar characteristic, together with a naturally high-strung and nervous action, enables it to assume its typical attitude when in position in the show cage, gripping the perch firmly and pulling itself up to its fullest possible height. At this stage the line of the back, from shoulder to the tip of the tail, should be completely perpendicular—this being an essential point of a show Belgian—but in contrast to the raising of the shoulders to their utmost height, the head is actually *depressed*, with the neck reaching out to its limit and the beak pointing directly downwards towards the bottom of the cage, and this position is held for several seconds at a time while the judge examines the exhibit.

Little or no scientific investigation is recorded as having been carried out upon the Belgian canary, but it is probable that its characteristic high shoulder, 'nervy' action and ability to hold a position are the results of mutation, which have been further developed by selective breeding and training to what some people might regard as unnatural limits.

The following is the Scale of Points of the Confederation Ornithologique Mondiale for the Belgian canary:

1. *POSITION*

POSITION (10 points): Comfortable and confident.
NECK (10 points): Fine and well elongated.
LEGS (4 points): Upright and stiff.
SHOULDERS (10 points): High.

SOOTY-BLACK CANARY. A recent breakthrough in canary inheritance, this new mutation is characterized by the presence of a great number of black feathers. It is a progeny of a Gloster Fancy canary cock which had earlier produced young with black feathers. It was bred in 1975, black deepened in color after first molt. Blacks birds were known in the London Fancy, but unfortunately this has become extinct.

BORDER FANCY CANARY. A wing marked yellow cock.

HEAD (6 points): Lowered.

2. *FORM*

HEAD (3 points): Small, oval, narrow and sleek.

NECK (10 points): Long, refined and extended.

SHOULDERS (10 points): High, well set and well filled.

BACK (5 points): Long, broad, well filled and upright.

BODY (5 points): Long and tapering.

BREAST (5 points): Prominent and well filled.

WINGS (5 points): Long, tightly folded, touching without crossing.

TAIL (3 points): Long, upright, closely folded, stiff and closed at the tip.

LEGS (4 points): Long, slim and upright.

PLUMAGE (6 points): Smooth, without frills.

SIZE (4 points): 17 to 18 cm. from the tip of the beak to the end of the tail.

TOTAL — 100 points

FRILLED CANARIES

The term 'frilled canaries' is here employed in a general way for, just as the expression 'crested canaries' can be used to embrace a number of breeds which possess this feature, frilled canaries also are to be found in several distinct varieties which differ from each other in varying degrees of type and size, and in the extent of the development of their frilled feathering which is their distinguishing characteristic. The chief varieties are the Parisian, Dutch and Italian Frills. The origin of the frilled feather formation is due to a mutation, generally thought to have occurred in the 'Old Dutch' canary at quite an early date and appears to have been well established in the Low Countries early in the nineteenth century. Frilled canaries were known throughout Europe originally by the general name of 'Dutch Canaries' until the emergence of distinct local variations on the basic type gave rise to other names.

The principal characteristic of all of the breeds is the curling of the feathers into a distinctive pattern which is fundamentally the same for each, namely (a) the 'mantle' formed by the feathers of the back being divided by a central parting and curling forward over each shoulder like a cape, (b) the 'jabot' (or 'craw,' or 'waistcoat') formed by the breast feathers curling inward toward the center in the form of a closed shell or frilly ruffle, and (c) the 'fins' formed by bunches of feathers above the thighs curling outwards and upwards around the wings. Further frills, or their absence, differentiate between the various breeds as also does their posture in the show cage. As a secondary characteristic all of them are of a somewhat highly-strung disposition, often with a nervous action of the legs.

The Parisian Frill: In this variety the most extreme development of the frills is to be found and, at one time, it was also the largest of all canary breeds, being between 7¾ and 8¼ inches in length. Present-day examples however do not measure up to this and very few exceed about 7 inches. The Parisian Frill should be robust in appearance and vigorous in action, showing plenty of bounce and vitality. The characteristic features which form its show points can be summarized under the headings of 'type,' 'position' and 'feather formation'. In type it is a long, slim bird after the manner of the old-style Yorkshire but, naturally, this is disguised to a large extent by the profusion of feathering with which its body is clothed. In position, the carriage of its body is upright, on long, supple legs and there is a pronounced and distinctive swagger in the bird's action. Feathering may vary from long, flowing, fine plumes to shorter, crisper ones with a tighter curling.

The three principal kinds of frill should readily be distinguished. The mantle should fall symmetrically from the central parting over each shoulder, its feathers being long and broad, thus adding to the bulk of the bird by giving the appearance of extra width across the shoulders. At shows those exhibits having good shoulder width will have an advantage over those which appear narrower in this respect. Sometimes the mantle extends well down the back towards the rump, which is considered an additional good point. The jabot must be double-sided—that is to say that the frills must come from each side of the breast to form a profuse, feathery ruffle, symmetrical in shape and meeting in the middle—not

YORKSHIRE CANARY. Poor feather quality is in evidence in this cinnamon variegated bird as can be seen by the "eyebrow" and looseness at the thighs.

NEST AND EGGS. A typical canary's nest built in a "nest pan." The usual clutch is four or five eggs.

swept to one side, as though blown by the wind, which disqualifies a bird as a show specimen. The two fins also must be symmetrically balanced by being of equal length on each side and should consist of long feathers which curl well up. A bird in which the fins do not balance is at a disadvantage and one which possesses a fin on one side only is not considered to be a show bird.

Apart from these main frills, there can also be seen a number of smaller decorations, all of which contribute to the general finish of the bird. On the head the feathers may curl down on one or both sides, forming eyebrows not unlike those of the crest-bred canary; or they may curl or roll upwards in the form of a slight hood or helmet, while a curving sweep of the facial feathers often gives a whiskered effect. On the neck there is a general collar of frilled feathers and, on the rump, the upper tail coverts fall away on each side of the base of the tail in a similar manner to those of a cock.

The wing and tail feathers must be long, even and regular without the defect of displaced flights in the wings or of a deeply forked tail; neither should the tail be carried in a raised position. On the legs the thigh joint may be covered with long feathers which also tend to obscure the shank to some extent (a type known as 'culotte,' or 'trousered') and at shows an exhibit of this kind will have preference over one in which the thighs are normally feathered with short, silky feathers. A final interesting characteristic of this breed is that the toe-nails also grow with a pronounced twist in them and these corkscrew-like toe-nails are an additional mark of quality.

The following is the Scale of Points of the Confederation Ornithologique Mondiale for the Parisian Frilled canary:

SIZE AND SHAPE (10 points): From 19 to 22 cm. Well built.

FEATHERING (10 points): Very even. Fine and long, or crisp and short.

POSITION (10 points): Well poised. Massive and symmetrical disposition of the feathers.

MANTLE (15 points): Abundant and well developed, with frills reaching almost to the rump.

BREAST FEATHERS (10 points): Double frills, well furnished and symmetrical.

FLANKS (10 points): Symmetrical with mantle and jabot. Rising well over the wings and shoulders.

HEAD AND NECK (8 points): Frills on the head of the 'calotte' or 'casquette' type. Perfect transition from head to body.

TAIL COVERTS (5 points): Falling evenly from the rump on either side.

WINGS (5 points): Long and close to the body.

LEGS AND FEET (5 points): Well developed. Nails like a corkscrew.

TAIL (4 points): Long and large. Ends of the quills in line.

CONDITION (8 points): Vigorous, with poise. General impression massive and symmetrical.

TOTAL — 100 points

The Dutch Frill: To the casual observer this breed may well be taken for a smaller version of the Parisian Frill but this should not be so, for the Dutch Frill has several features which differ in detail from the Parisian. To begin with, it is a much smaller bird, being about 6½ to 6¾ inches in length, and is much less densely feathered. Too heavy frilling, in fact, is considered a fault and greater importance is attached to the regularity and symmetry of the frills. It has a small neat head, without any curled feathers, and a neck which is again free from frilling and clearly visible instead of being obscured by the mass of breast and collar feathers. The mantle is neat and nicely proportioned and without the additional tufting extending down to the rump such as is seen in the best of the Parisians. At the rear end of the bird, too, absence of heavy feathering is noticeable; the rump and vent are smoothly covered, and the long thigh joints are normally feathered. In position it stands well up on its long, somewhat stilty legs and shows plenty of 'nerve' and alertness.

One of the difficulties in breeding these birds arises from the fact that the Parisian and Dutch Frills have frequently been crossed in the past, so that many birds that are intermediate in character are in existence, and from many seem-

RED FACTOR CANARY. The opal mutation first occurred among Roller canaries in Germany but has now breed bred into most color forms including this frosted bronze opal cock.

BORDER FANCY CANARY. A self blue. As can be seen the "blue" is really more of a slate-grey with quite a mixture of brown.

Although not a particularly good specimen, this Frilled canary shows the disposition of the basic frills, the "craw" on the breast, the "fins" above the thighs and the "mantle" coming over the shoulders.

ingly good matings it is possible to raise youngsters of both types. It is only by following a rigid breeding policy, segregating the divergent types, and eliminating those that are not required, that this problem will be overcome.

The following is the Scale of Points of the Confederation Ornithologique Mondiale for the Dutch Frilled canary:

LEGS AND FEET (10 points):   Long thighs, normally feathered, legs not too bent.

HEAD AND NECK (15 points): Small and without frills, slightly raised.

SIZE (10 points): About 17 centimeters.

MANTLE (15 points): Symmetrical, well proportioned, without any additional frilling.

FLANKS (15 points): Full, bulky, even, rising towards the shoulders.

BREAST (15 points): Frills symmetrical and complete.

CONDITION (10 points): Healthy, çlean and entire.

PLUMAGE (10 points): Frills undamaged and symmetrical.

TOTAL — 100 points

The Italian Humpback Frill: This breed, known generally on the continent as the *Gibber Italicus*, is a creation of Italian fanciers. Although its precise origins are uncertain it appears to have arisen as an offshoot from another frilled breed (the *Southern* Dutch Frill, or Belgian Frill, to distinguish it from the original Dutch Frill of the north a variety once popular in the region of Naples, Caserte and Benevente, but now rather a rarity. The Southern Dutch Frill combined the frilled feathering characteristic with a typical posture not unlike that of the Scotch Fancy, and the Gibber, too, has a posture in the show cage in the form of a figure seven which is reminiscent of the Belgian. This similarity of form would seem to suggest a close relationship although the Gibber is a smaller bird.

Its very small, slight frame may have been brought about partly by inbreeding but more probably by the continued use of double yellow matings which has produced a bird that is lightly built, small of stature, and with short,

LIZARD CANARY. The oldest of all canary breeds. This clear-capped gold shows well the breast markings but little can be seen of the "spangling" on the back.

Just independent — two young green canaries newly weaned.

crisp and scanty plumage. All birds of this variety are yellows, there are no buffs, a distinction shared by no other
breed of canary. (See the chapter on Breeding Theory on the
subject of homozygous yellows.) If the feathering were to be
too long and abundant, two of the notable characteristics of
the breed, namely its naked sternum and naked thighs,
would no longer be in evidence.

The following is the Scale of Points of the Confederation
Ornithologique Mondiale for the Gibber Italicus:

POSITION (20 points): In the form of a figure seven.
HEAD (6 points): Small and fine, narrow skull, small beak,
    no frills.
NECK (15 points): Long and horizontal, no frills.
LEGS (15 points): Long and stiff, thighs exposed.
WINGS (6 points): Long and close to the body.
SHOULDERS (10 points): High, with symmetrical frills.
TAIL (6 points): Long, vertical, pressed to the perch.
BREAST (10 points): Breastbone naked, frills not meeting in
    the center.
FLANKS (6 points): Symmetrical on both sides, holding the
    wings.
LENGTH (6 points):
TOTAL — 100 points

Other breeds coming from Italy include the *Paduan
Frill*, which is similar to the Parisian but with a crest on the
head, and the *Milan Frill*, also known as the color frill.
There are, or rather have been, several other races of frills
such as the *Munich Frill*, the *Swiss Frill* and others, but the
differences between them all are so slight as to make positive
identification difficult and their claim to be regarded as genuine breeds would seem to be somewhat tenuous. Non-frilled
breeds are very few and without much of a following. They
include the *Bernese*, which might be described as a large
Roller with the stance of the Yorkshire, and the *German
Crest*, which again may be regarded as a crested Roller, usually coming in Red Factor colors.

18

Canaries in North America

BY DR. VAL CLEAR

There is great parallel between the canary fancy in North America and the fancy in Great Britain. Most canaries in the new world came from stock that was originally British —some after having spent a few intermediate generations in Continental Europe or Japan.

Except for the unusual feather-texture specialties such as the frills, and the songsters such as the Rollers, Waterslagers, and Timbrados, most other varieties of canaries were created in the United Kingdom. The preferred breeding stock still comes from there and the official standards are lifted almost *verbatim* from corresponding British associations.

There are three major interests among canary fanciers in North America, as in Britain. There are those whose main enthusiasm is for the singing varieties, those who breed for body conformation (type), and those whose prime concern is color. These categories are more distinct on paper than in practice, however; most fanciers actually keep birds of other kinds even though they may specialize in one type more than the others.

At the Twenty-seventh National Cage Bird Exhibition in 1975 there were 640 different classes scheduled for canaries, not counting American Singers, which use a different system for competing. Although the classification system was perhaps a bit more detailed than some of the annual state and regional shows, the outline of classes used would be approximately the same as the National's. Most of the following classifications would be divided into four separate classes for Old Cock, Young Cock, Old Hen, and Young Hen, and as many as twelve different color classes for each of these.

NEW COLOR CANARY. A melanin dilute cinnamon (or melanin
pastel) yellow ground bird. Compare this with the same mutation in
the Red Factor series.

RED FACTOR CANARY. In the 'self' birds, red orange and apricot feathering is still to be found and is known as non-frosted and frosted. This example is of a non-frosted melanin pastel.

1. BORDER FANCY CANARIES
2. TYPE CANARIES
   Yorkshire
   Norwich Plainhead
   Gloster Fancy Corona
   Gloster Fancy Consort
   Columbus Fancy Crested
   Columbus Fancy Plainhead
   Crested Norwich
   Crestbred Norwich
   Lizard
   Frill
   Any Other Type
3. DOMESTIC HARTZ CANARIES
   Domestic Hartz Plainhead
   Domestic Hartz Topknot
4. AMERICAN SINGER CANARIES
   Old American Singer
   Young American Singer
   American Singer Hen
5. COLOR BRED LIPOCHROMES
   First-cross Hybrid
   Second-cross Hybrid
   Red-orange, Non-frost
   Red-orange, Frost
   Red-ground Dimorphic Hens and Rose-Ivory
   Color Bred Border Cross
   Color Bred Crested
6. COLOR BRED MELANINS
   Red-orange Ground Color
   Yellow Ground Color
   Dominant White Ground Color
   Opal
        Red-orange Ground
        Yellow Ground
        White Ground
   Greywing, Ino, and Melanin Dimorphic Hen

Variegated Border Fancy canary.

BORDER FANCY CANARY. A nice self green. Border breeders are keen on a bird that is as near to grass green as possible.

YORKSHIRE CANARY. The blue variegated white bird seen in other photographs shows particularly well the offending twisted feathers around the throat.

There are over thirty different categories of canary in the preceding list, a good catalogue of the kinds of canaries that are being bred in North America in enough numbers to merit a class in the National Exhibition. It should be pointed out that there are also some minor varieties that have not yet been recognized by the managers of the Exhibition, such as the Japanese Hoso and the Miniature Yorkshire, and that in time these may find their way into the limelight as well.

JUDGING ROLLERS

Each national specialist society (such as that for Yorkshires or for Lizards) sets its own standard and in most cases it is identical to the British formula for the same variety. There is one notable exception to this, the standard used by Roller judges.

Two different standards are used for judging Rollers in North America, one British and the other North American. When the announcement of the competition is published it is customary to indicate the point system to be used. The British Scale of Points is as follows:

Hollow Roll	10
Bass	10
Water Glucke	10
Glucke	10
Glucke Roll	10
Hollow Bell	8
Schockel	8
Flutes	6
Water Roll	6
Deep Bubbling Water Tour	5
Bell Roll	.3
Bell Tour	2
General Effect	10

The One Hundred Point Standard popular in the United States and Canada varies from the preceding in certain respects:

Hollow Roll	18
Bass	18
Hollow Bell	12
Schockel	12
Glucke	12
Flutes	9
Water Tours	9
Bells	3
Bell Tours	3
General Effects	4

JUDGING THE DOMESTIC HARTZ

The Domestic Hartz is a convenient classification in any show. There is no standard provided for judging, and little agreement among fanciers or judges as to what is most desirable in the birds. It is a miscellaneous class and some fanciers claim that it is a catch-all into which birds gravitate who have insufficient quality to compete in other divisions.

Since there is no written standard by which Domestic Hartz birds are judged, there tends to be a major emphasis on condition. The better birds tend to be of pleasing proportions, attractively colored, and in excellent condition, but a bird that wins under one judge may fail to place under another. There usually is a separate class structure for crested varieties, since crested birds require special attention to their crests.

How did the term "Domestic Hartz" come about? Opinions of fanciers differ, but it seems likely that it is rooted in the original term for canary singers in this country, "Hartz Mountain Canaries," which carried no physical type standard. The only consideration was (and still is) the song. Since the new American variety likewise had no physical standard it was simple to draw a parallel and call these "Domestic" Hartz, meaning bred to appeal to the fancier's ear as well as to his eye, and developed in the United States.

Some Domestic Hartz are birds bred by fanciers who merely produce birds that appeal to their own tastes. Others are birds of pleasing conformation but not sufficiently true in type standard for the Border or the Columbus Fancy. In

NEW COLOR CANARY. Recessive white—a variegated bird, not favored among fanciers who prefer them either self or clear.

either case, they are generally satisfactory birds for the consumer not especially concerned with a highly bred bird with impressive credentials. No attempt is made to judge their singing ability, however; that function is reserved solely for the Rollers or the American Singers.

THE COLUMBUS FANCY

Several decades ago a new variety of canary was developed among fanciers in Ohio. Later termed "Columbus Fancy," because its most enthusiastic protagonists lived near the city of that name, it has now been accepted sufficiently so that classes are provided in many state shows and in the National Exhibition.

There are varying versions of what transpired during the early stages of development of the new breed, but apparently the Lancashire Coppy and Border were used, with additional in-put from Gloster and Norwich canaries. Although the breed is definitely established, it is more difficult to produce good birds consistently than with other varieties.

The Columbus Fancy occurs in all color variations except red. Although the color of the crest is not specified in the standard, it is usually black. As with crested breeds, the standard is written in two versions, with and without the crest. The reason for this is that two crested birds normally are not mated to each other; to do so is to risk bald offspring. Crested are mated to non-crested. Since the latter is as important as the former in production of winning birds, standards are needed for both.

Crested Columbus Fancy

Crest (size, shape, droop; size of a half-dollar, round rosette)	45
Body	10
Feather	10
Position	10
Condition	10
Beak	5
Neck (fullness)	5
Legs (short, thighs well clothed)	5
	100

Smooth-head Columbus Fancy

Head (large, well rounded)	25
Body (stout, chubby; 5½-6" long)	20
Eyebrows	10
Beak (short, neat)	10
Feather (leafy texture)	10
Size, shape, position over perch	15
Health, cleanliness	10
	100

DEVELOPING THE AMERICAN SINGER CANARY

It takes many years to produce a new breed of canary, and a number of determined fanciers. There had been discussions earlier, but in 1934 several fanciers decided to organize the effort to develop a new kind of canary that would be aimed at the preferences of North Americans. What they wanted was a bird that would sing freely under normal household conditions, and a song that was louder than a Roller's and softer than a Chopper's.

By 1943 there had been such progress both in breeding the birds and in mustering support among fanciers that the American Singer Club was founded. They proposed to blend the Border Fancy Canary and the German Roller Canary in such a way as to produce a songster that is (in the words of the official definition) "a song-type canary bred in the United States by a systematic plan known as the blending of Roller to Border Fancy over a period of years to produce a canary bird that has (1) an outstanding, free, harmonious song, pleasing to the ear, neither too loud nor too harsh, with plenty of variety; (2) a beautiful shape or type not over 5¾ inches long, with tight feather that will please the average home lover of canaries."

No other association provides a carefully worked-out genetic chart such as the American Singers Club gives its members. The goal is to have a strain of birds that are 69% Roller and 31% Border Fancy. To get there from scratch takes at least five years of faithful pairing of succeeding generations in a deliberate plain of line breeding. Most new fanciers now start with stock purchased from seasoned fanciers who have those five years well behind them.

The ideal American Singer, then, is a planned blend of two existing varieties. But it has a distinctiveness all its own. It has a medium-sized beak; a rounded head; pronounced shoulders; medium-length tail, wings, and leg; and all this on a small body. It should not have the Roller's "dance" on the perch while singing, but should stand on the perch at an angle between 35° and 45°; and most important of all, should be of fearless disposition.

All colors that exist among Rollers and Borders are also seen among American Singers. Introducing a special color such as Red Factor has implications for line breeding operations, and the fanciers who attempt it need a couple of extra years to produce a solid strain. But color is merely a personal preference; no difference is recognized by judges.

JUDGING AMERICAN SINGERS

Rollers are usually judged as teams of birds entered by the same fancier, so that it is a team that competes with the team entered by another fancier. American Singers are entered individually and are placed into competitive groups in such a way that two birds from the same owner do not compete against each other except in the final stages of the contest.

Part of the training of the American Singer is to sing freely despite commotion, so that after he is moved from the stands to the judging bench the bird has only ten minutes in which to perform for the judge. If he does not his cage is labeled "N.S." (for "No Song") and he is, in effect, out of the competition.

The standard is as follows:

Freedom of Song	10
Rendition of Song	60
Conformation of body	20
Condition	10

Cages used in the shows are what are usually termed shelf cages, which are small, rectangular, and with one solid end. Club rules vary, but usually the floor is covered with gravel. There are three perches to permit the bird some movement as he performs for the judge.

The song must be neither Chopper nor Roller; too much of either is a weakness. No more than six "chops" in a song are permitted. To enter official competition the bird must have been bred by the exhibitor and wear a band issued by the National American Singers Club.

THE NATIONAL ASSOCIATION

Fanciers dedicated to American Singers seem to have an unusually strong *esprit de corps*. They sense a special belongingness to each other which was born in their struggle to establish the new breed of canary. Their number and their enthusiasm are increasing steadily. At state, regional, and national shows they constitute a noticeable minority. They provide valuable services to new members in the form of guides to breeding and suggestions for successful production of qualified American Singers.

Most of the national specialist societies run a monthly listing in *American Cage-bird Magazine,* and this includes the National American Singers Club. Interested persons can secure the name and address of the current secretary of any of the clubs by writing for a copy of the magazine at 3449 North Western Avenue, Chicago, Illinois 60618.

19

The Red Factor and other New Colors

What may well prove to be the most significant developments in the canary fancy have occurred during the present century in the field of color breeding, and it is not improbable that the fancier of the future may regard the lists of color varieties of today much as we look back upon those of Hervieux. Just as some of the early mutations listed by this authority have either been completely lost or, like the cinnamon, become an integral part of most of the modern type breeds so, almost certainly, will some of the present day colors eventually be accepted by fanciers, while others will be destined for obscurity and excite little interest except among experimental breeders.

Color breeding as an end in itself is, in fact, quite a new conception in the fancy. The canary was originally kept for its song, and later became the object of improvement by fanciers into various exhibition forms; but concentration upon color for its own sake is a phenomenon of this century which has appealed particularly to scientifically-minded fanciers, who are able to follow the new developments through their knowledge of genetics.

TYPE

Some of the new color varieties are due to the action of a single mutated gene, and as such could very easily be bred into any of the standard types of canary in the same way as the cinnamon or dominant white. Other colors however, are the result of the interaction of several genes both of a primary and modifying nature, which are not easily transferred in a body to any standard breed. It is for this reason perhaps that type breeders have not been interested so far in the introduction of new colors into their stocks. Conversely, the color breeders have had no desire to hinder their own work by attempting to standardize their birds into any particular type.

The following are representative of the better known color varieties dealt with, as far as is possible, in chronological order.

THE DILUTE

Color breeding originated in Holland where, in 1900, P.J. Helder bred what he described as a pale, ash-grey hen from an ordinary green x green mating. Breeding tests showed the new characteristic to be recessive and sex-linked in its behavior, and its visual effect was to reduce the intensity of the melanin pigments in the plumage to something like half their normal color value. The variety was given the name 'Agate,' as it was deemed to be the reappearance of a lost mutation—the agate canary as listed by Hervieux in 1709. In Britain and America however, it became more aptly known as 'Dilute,' being descriptive of its effect upon the melanin color pigments.

Because of its simple mode of inheritance it is easily allied to any of the existing self colored melanins in the form of dilute green, dilute cinnamon, dilute blue or dilute fawn, and although a clear canary can genetically be a dilute it cannot exhibit the characteristic in its plumage, owing to the absence of variegation factors. It is therefore useless to breed this variety in anything but self colors.

Owing to its rather pale 'washed-out' appearance the dilute has never found many admirers, except perhaps when allied to the red factor series, but it is of interest historically having been instrumental in giving rise to an interest in color breeding.

THE RECESSIVE WHITE

This mutation occurred simultaneously in England and New Zealand in the year 1908, the breeders being W. Keisel of London and Miss Lee of Martinborough. Subsequently the English strain became extinct, so that the recessive whites of today are descendants of the New Zealand mutation.

Genetically this variety is quite different from the dominant white, and it can also be distinguished visually by being devoid of any lipochrome in the plumage, whereas the dominant whites show just a faint tinge of yellow on the outer edges of the primary flight feathers.

Being a homozygous characteristic the recessive white breeds true and, when mated white x white, 100 per cent white youngsters are produced, as a double dose of this gene is not lethal as is the case with the dominant white. If mated to canaries of normal ground color the recessive white disappears in the first cross, but the intermating of two 'carriers' can bring about its reappearance in the next generation. Since recessive white is a ground color the melanin pigments are not affected, and will appear as blue or fawn if variegation is present.

Birds of this color variety had a brief period of importance when it was thought that through them the red canary might be achieved, but since this assumption has been proved ill-founded they have lapsed into obscurity, and now relatively few are to be obtained.

THE DOMINANT WHITE

Coming from Germany sometime after 1918, this color variety was soon available in fair numbers and was eventually bred into most of the standard exhibition types by fanciers, since when it has ceased to be of any further interest to color breeders as such. The genetics involved in the breeding of dominant whites was fully dealt with in the chaper on Breeding Theory.

THE RED FACTOR

By far the most important of the new colors is the Red Factor canary which has now achieved the status of a major exhibition variety. It may be regarded ostensibly as the by-product of experimental breeding in search of a red canary, for although there are several breeders who are still pursuing that particular objective, the great majority are now breeding the Red Factor purely as an exhibition bird.

History: From the early years of the century following the publication of Mendel's *Principles of Heredity*, research into the problems of inheritance in the canary was carried out by various geneticists, among them Dr. Hans Duncker in Germany. In 1929, as a result of his investigations, he published a theory on how it should be possible, eventually, to produce a true red canary by introducing into the normal canary's genetical make-up a factor responsible for red feather pigmentation.

Fertile hybrids between the brilliant vermilion Venezuelan hooded siskin (*Spinus cuculatus*) and the canary had been confirmed on several occasions before this date, and indeed a strain of canaries of hybrid origin had already been produced, also in Germany, by Bruno Matern, but it is really through Dr. Duncker's published work that impetus was first given to the quest for a red canary. In general however, the idea did not at first appeal to fanciers in England, the traditional stronghold of 'type' canaries, as much as it did to those in continental Europe and in the U.S.A., but the few whose imagination had been fired were to make an important contribution to progress.

In addition to Dr. Duncker other pioneer workers included Dr. C.B. Bennett in the U.S.A. (a study on the nature of the Orange canary) and A.K. Gill in England, who gained international repute in this field, and whose book *New Coloured Canaries* remains the standard work today. It was he who bred the first Red Factor canaries in England from birds sent to him by Dr. Duncker as early as 1928.

It was first assumed, following the experiences with dilutes, recessive and dominant whites, that it would be a relatively simple matter to transfer the 'red factor' (i.e. the gene responsible for red coloration) from the hooded siskin to the canary, through the medium of the proved fertile F1 copper hybrid; but this did not prove to be the case. Various complications arose which caused Dr. Duncker to amend his original theory, and it was eventually discovered that the red of the hooded siskin was not produced by one simply-heritable gene but by the interaction of many, including one that in fact produced yellow! Another obstacle that impeded progress was the infertility of the hens from the hooded siskin x canary cross, so that back-crossing copper hybrids to canary hens was the only method open to the experimentalists. Finally, after three generations of such back-crossing, fertile hens were obtainable.

Many years of patient work followed which included selective breeding from the deepest colored birds and repeated re-introductions of hooded siskin 'blood,' but so far the red canary has not materialized, although some of the very best examples are certainly of a deep reddish-orange.

It will be appreciated that the whole breed of Red Factor canaries that have evolved from this work owe part of their heredity to the canary and part to the hooded siskin. Technically they are not pure canaries but a strain of fertile hybrids, but since they will interbreed freely with any existing variety of true canary and produce completely fertile young, they can for practical purposes be considered as canaries.

Description: Red Factor canaries owe their color partly to the red genes inherited from the hooded siskin and partly to the yellow genes inherited from both the canary and the hooded siskin, so that from the interaction of these a plumage of some shade of orange is produced. In inferior specimens this may be relatively pale, but in the better ones it can be quite an intense reddish-orange not far short of certain types of red.

The usual two categories of feather structure are to be found in this breed, but as the terms 'yellow' and 'buff' are obviously misnomers when used in connection with orange colored birds, other terms have been adopted as alternatives. These include 'red orange' and 'apricot,' 'non frosted' and 'frosted,' and 'intensive' and 'non-intensive.'

The majority of Red Factor canaries have been bred by fanciers in the clear form, but variegated specimens are available and among certain sections of the fancy self colored birds are favored. These red orange greens and red orange cinnamons can be of a wonderful color, as also can their dilute counterparts, the red orange dilute green and the red orange dilute cinnamon, for it must be remembered that the red 'factor' is present as a ground color only and has no effect upon the melanin pigments, so that when these are superimposed upon the red orange background some very attractive red-bronze or glowing copper effects are produced.

The breeding of Red Factors has until recently been directed along one channel only—the pursuit of color, and the rejection by fanciers of any attempt to divert their attention to the production of a particular type, has led to great progress being made since the early days. As a result of this the Red Factor has tended to develop into a rather nondescript type of bird, which owes its form in part to the hooded siskin and in part to the canaries in its ancestry. It is, nevertheless, an attractive little bird which can take its place with credit among other small breeds of canary.

Breeding: The breeders of Red Factors have been rather less circumscribed by the traditional yellow x buff matings (red orange x apricot in their case) as used in other breeds of canary, since the sole basis for the selection of their breeding pairs has been that of redness of color. At one time red orange x red orange matings were much in vogue, and they often gave rise to birds with quite intense coloring but, as was perhaps to be expected, frequently at the expense of feather quality (see the remarks upon homozygous yellows in Chapter 6). Subsequently apricot x apricot mating was practiced a good deal, especially when it was appreciated that, although not so intense in color, these birds had less visual yellow in their plumage which consequently was often of a decidedly pinkish hue. These matings also had their disadvantages by increasing the amount of frosting, so that nowadays, when well colored birds of both feather types are available, it is almost universal for most matings to be of the traditional red orange x apricot type, and this is certainly the best method for the beginner to adopt, at least until some experience has been gained.

Molting: The molting of Red Factors presents an interesting problem, not found in normal yellow canaries, the basis of which concerns the biochemistry involved in the production of red pigment in the feathers.

It had long been known to aviculture that the coloring of birds with red plumage tended to fade in captivity, until research into the chemical structure of the red pigment showed that this was largely due to the absence of certain carotenoid substances in the diet during the molting period. If this deficiency was rectified the bird was enabled to produce the true intensity of its red plumage.

Until this was properly understood breeders continued to feed their birds the same diet as they would to a yellow canary, and in so doing were unwittingly depriving them of the very items of food that were necessary for the red genes to express themselves. At this period even the specialist societies forbade the use of anything other than the usual molting diet of seed, soft food and greenstuff. Eventually however, when convinced of the illogicality of this procedure, they permitted the use of any vegetable preparation containing the essential carotenes.

This means that during the molt most breeders nowadays feed their birds one of the color feeding preparations containing *canthaxanthin*, which has been found to produce the reddest color, at the same time excluding any items containing *lutein*, which is a strong source of yellow pigmentation. This is mainly present in many green vegetables, in egg yolk and in certain seeds especially rape, thistle and hemp. Of the basic carbohydrate seeds, oats contain only about half the quantity of lutein as canary or millet, and as a result many Red Factor breeders use a seed mixture of groats and niger instead of the usual canary and rape seed. For fresh vegetables as a source of vitamin C, greenstuff is replaced by carrot in unlimited quantity and egg yolk is omitted as a source of protein from any soft food preparations.

Exhibiting: Not being a breed of type or position the Red Factor needs no specialized training for exhibition. The bird however should be quite steady and not flutter about when the show cage is being handled by the judge otherwise it may be at a disadvantage in close competition.

The peculiar quality of the red pigmentation in the plumage of this breed can really be seen accurately only in good, natural light, and should certainly be judged under such conditions—a point that show promoting societies unfortunately do not always appreciate. Artificial lighting, especially of the fluorescent daylight type, 'kills' the glowing color of Red Factors to a considerable degree, so that at many exhibitions they are not to be seen at their best.

THE DIMORPHIC

As a result of the hybridizing that was used in the creation of the Red Factor canary it is perhaps not surprising that genes, other than those responsible for red coloring, should have been handed down from the hooded siskin to some of its descendants. One of these genetic factors is responsible for the characteristic of *sexual dimorphism*—a condition common to many species of bird (but not the canary), in which male and female have quite different plumage patterns. The hen hooded siskin for example, instead of possessing the brilliant coloring of the male, is of a uniform slate-grey with the exception of a reddish flush on the wing butts, breast and rump, and these characteristic markings have been perpetuated in certain canary hens of the Red Factor breed, which as a result have been termed 'dimorphics'.

In the clear form these hens are mainly off-white in color, but show orange pigmentation at exactly the same 'points' as the hooded siskin hen. The majority of breeders at first ignored them as being poorly colored examples of apricot, but about 1930 Bruno Matern used dimorphic hens to mate to his best colored cock birds, following a theory that because they had inherited this essential character from the hooded siskin they might also be carrying other useful siskin genes for the production of red. He was in fact very successful in founding a strain of deep-colored birds which he christened 'carmines,' and as a result, a craze for using dimorphic hens followed.

Nowadays it is generally accepted, following a good deal of breeding experience, that a dimorphic hen does not necessarily produce redder young—i.e. through the mere fact of being a dimorphic—but is only as good as her genotype, the same as any normal Red Factor hen.

These dimorphic hens are quite attractive little birds in their own right and many breeders still like to keep one or two, especially as a class is usually provided for them at the larger shows of new colored canaries. Quite recently a new form of dimorphism has occurred and the mutation has been given the name of *New Dimorphic*. It differs from the old type in that the cocks as well as the hens possess the typical dimorphic hen pattern of plumage. In the Red Factor these can be quite beautiful birds with a chalk-white body, red at the usual points of rump and wing butts, and having a distinctive red facial 'blaze' rather similar in appearance to the European goldfinch. This mutation originated in Italy from birds of English Gloster Fancy ancestry and was first identified by the French canary color expert, M. Ascheri.

THE CITRON

This color variety may have been in existence for some time without attracting any attention, but with the extension of interest in color breeding it has recently come to the notice of breeders. Although as yet imperfectly understood, the citron canary is stated by some experts to possess an 'optical blue' factor which gives it a somewhat greenish tinge, as distinct from the more usual golden or daffodil yellows encountered in normal canaries. As their appearance is only a little different from ordinary yellow varieties, citrons have excited small interest except among the experimentalists, who see in them the possibility of producing a true blue canary instead of the present blues, which really are more or less slate colored.

RECENT MUTATIONS

Several interesting new mutations which show considerable promise for the future have occurred on the continent in recent years. Nomenclature is regrettably still somewhat confused as they are often known by different names in various countries but, until standardization has been agreed upon, the following are well understood in English-speaking countries.

The Opal: This mutation is said to have occurred in Germany in 1949, among a stock of Roller canaries. It has been variously referred to as the 'German Opal,' the 'German Pastel,' and in Germany itself as the 'Free-transmitting' or 'Free Dilute,' on account of the genetical nature of the mutant gene. In effect, this bird is a *non* sex-linked dilute but differs from the older type of dilute canary by being very much paler in the dilution of the melanin pigments.

The Lipochrome Pastel: Apart from the two types of white, this is the first direct mutation ever to affect the lipochrome (ground) colors of the canary. It appeared in Holland among Red Factor canaries probably in 1949, since the first two specimens to be exhibited were shown by the pioneer color breeder P.J. Helder in 1950, shortly before his death. This mutation produces a dilution and levelling out of the lipochrome throughout the entire plumage to a delightful pastel shade, which in yellow birds is termed 'Ivory Pastel' and in Red Factors, 'Rose Pastel'. The latter is truly a pale shade of rose pink and quite unique among canaries. The pastel characteristic is recessive and sex-linked in its manner of inheritance, and should of course be bred only in clear birds to see its full effect.

The Melanin Pastel: In 1960 in Holland, Messrs. Kollen and Brokmeyer discovered a dilute Red Factor hen in which the melanin pigment was so pale as to be of a uniform light brown color throughout, without any pencilling being visible at all. From this mutation has been bred a new color variety which has been called the 'Melanin Pastel,' since its effect upon the melanin pigments is roughly the same as the Lipochrome Pastel upon the ground colors, but apart from their similar mode of inheritance which is recessive and sex-linked, they appear to be unconnected and can be inherited independently.

The Ino: Canaries with red eyes were mentioned by Hervieux over 270 years ago but, apart from the so-called pink-eye of the cinnamon which, in fact is more of a plum color, none have been seen since—that is, until the advent of the 'Ino' mutation about 1967. This distinctive red-eyed form has been given the name of 'rubino' in Red Factors, 'lutino' in yellow-ground birds, and 'albino' in white-ground. Apart from the eye color, in this mutation apparently there is a powerful melanin dilution factor present which has a variable effect upon the various melanins, removing completely all traces of black and reducing the intensity of the brown. In some cases this can produce what appears to be a completely clear bird, although still a true self as can be determined by its pigmented underflue, and in others what has been described as a 'hammered copper' effect. Genetically the Ino is recessive and non sex-linked to normal pigmentation but its relationship to other mutant forms has yet to be determined.

The Satinette: This, the newest of the color mutations, appeared in Holland in 1971 and, like the Ino, is a red-eyed bird. Apart from the fact that it also possesses a strong melanin dilution element the full effects of this have not yet been studied in detail. However, it is apparent that in some forms it can produce a virtually clear bird but with faint brownish markings on the back that give a most delicate effect. The Satinette is another recessive sex-linked mutation.

With so much happening in the world of color breeding and a continuing tendency for new mutations to appear, the keen fancier should be at no loss to find a wide range of interests which will keep him in the forefront of developments in the canary world.

20

The Roller

In the majority of text books on canaries, the Roller, if it is dealt with at all, is usually relegated to the final chapter. In view of the fact that it is specially bred for the very virtue for which the canary was first prized, namely its song, this may, perhaps, be something of an injustice. It is however, more a matter of convenience to segregate it from the remainder, since all other breeds are essentially visual in their appeal, and are loosely termed 'type' canaries, whereas in the Roller, appearance counts for nothing and it is the song instead that has been cultivated to the highest degree of perfection. It is the continuous and melodious rolling delivery of this song that has given the breed its popular name.

HISTORY

Inasmuch as the canary was originally valued and imported on account of its song, the Roller may perhaps be said to have had its origins in the very earliest days—at least with regard to the concept in men's minds of the species being primarily important for its singing ability. The cultured voice of the modern Roller however, is as far removed from the song of the wild canary as the differences in appearance that exist between the highly-developed exhibition varieties and the ancestral type, and it is principally to the breeders in Germany that we owe the changes that have been made.

As long ago as 1678, in Ray's translation of Willughby's *Ornithology*, an English writer (Josiah Blagrove) is quoted as saying, "Canary birds of late years have been brought abundantly out of Germany. . . and these German birds in handsomeness and song excel those brought out of the Canaries," which would suggest that even at that early date some thought had been given to selection on the basis of song. But the true beginnings of the Roller as we now know it belong to the eighteenth century, with the idea of actually training the birds to sing in an approved manner instead of leaving the matter to chance.

The original locality where this specialized branch of canary culture was practiced was the Hartz Mountains, and more particularly, in the town of St. Andreasburg, where at one time it was said that some 400 families were engaged in what was later to become a very profitable industry.

It was noticed early that some canaries had an exceptionally good ear and a faculty for mimicry which made them capable of assimilating the song passages of other birds into their own, and often the nightingale, woodlark and other acknowledged European songsters were made use of as tutors for the most promising birds. Later, musical instruments such as the flute were employed to improve the range and quality of the song, and ultimately an ingenious device known as a bird organ was invented, which was able to produce continuous trilling, rolling and bubbling notes as required. By careful training and the selection of the most accomplished birds for breeding purposes, strains of these artificial songsters were gradually developed which later became the basis of a considerable export trade from Germany to other parts of Europe and the Americas. At the height of the trade it was estimated that quite half a million birds left Germany each year for various parts of the world.

The vast majority of these birds were probably destined to be household pets, much as the budgerigar is today, and since they were so cheaply bought and replaced extensive breeding of them was not to be expected. There were some, of course, to whom it did make an appeal, and to such men must be acknowledged the credit for establishing the Roller canary. But at the same time it must be admitted that in the early days they little appreciated the true merit of the bird's performance, and singing competitions frequently took place on a time basis, with the winner being merely the contestant that sang for the greatest length of time!

With the continued importation of the choicest birds available, aided by the formation of various Roller clubs, a steady improvement in standards took place from the early years of the present century onwards, and today our leading birds at least are not outclassed by the continental performers, and stock of high quality is available at very reasonable prices.

DESCRIPTION

With song being the sole basis for selection, the appearance of the Roller has altered little over the years from that of the original wild canary, the great majority of them being of a nondescript type and either self green, foul or variegated in marking. This matters nothing to the true Roller fancier however, for it is only the song that counts. Nevertheless in recent years, possibly in an effort to make surplus stock more attractive to the general public, some attempt has been made to introduce other colors, so that clear yellow, orange or white Rollers are now available, although they are alleged to be inferior as songsters.

To attempt the description of bird song in words is acknowledged to be a difficult task which at best can only give a general impression, but if taken in conjunction with a recording, or better still with a live performance, it can help to explain some of the technicalities of the various passages that make up the Roller's song.

To begin with, it must be appreciated that the song of a fully trained contest Roller is as different from that of the ordinary 'type' canary as is the voice of an operatic star performing an aria when compared with an untrained singer. The song comes from the throat and is delivered through an almost closed beak, so that at all times the volume is restrained and well controlled, never too loud and often being no more than a whisper. The bird never gives vent to the noisy, rollicking 'chop-chop-chop' type of song associated with the ordinary canary, and in fact any harsh, jarring, shrill or over-loud notes are detrimental to a good performance, and may be marked as faults against the singer.

The British song standard recognizes thirteen well-defined song passages called 'rolls' and 'tours,' each of which constitutes a distinct melodic entity, although few, if any, birds are capable of uttering all of them. In any case it is not necessarily the extent of the bird's repertoire that counts in its favor but the degree of perfection with which it performs the various passages, especially the more difficult, higher scoring ones. Each tour has a recognized name, often the original German one where this is not easily rendered in translation, which is more or less descriptive of the sounds being produced. The chief of these are 'Hollow Roll,' 'Bass Roll,' 'Bell Roll,' 'Water Roll,' 'Glucke,' 'Water Glucke,' 'Glucke Roll,' 'Flutes,' 'Schockel,' 'Hollow Bell,' 'Bell' and 'Deep Bubbling Water.'

The various rolls, as their name implies, are delivered in a continuous rolling or trilling manner, somewhat reminiscent in tempo of the purring of a kitten (though not of course in tone), and may be imitated in a general way by whistling a note and at the same time vibrating the tongue rapidly behind the upper teeth thus: *whrrrrrrrrr, trrrrrrrrr* or *srrrrrrrrr*. The lower notes would be in the compass of Bass Roll and then, progressing up the scale, they would constitute Hollow Roll, finally reaching Bell Roll in the higher register.

In some other tours it is possible to distinguish a distinct beating of the notes rather than the faster trilling effect of the rolls, and these in general may be expressed thus: *lululululu, glooglooglooglooo*, etc., the keen ear being able to detect different consonants and vowels according to the tour being sung.

The remaining tours may best be described as composite ones in which the rolling and beating notes are incorporated into a simultaneous rendering, often giving the most beautiful effect, as, for example, in Glucke Roll, and if instead of being delivered 'dry' the effect is liquid, as of water rippling in a stream, the various water tours are produced.

The ultimate beauty of the Roller's song lies not only in the rendering of the various tours in as perfect a manner as possible, but in the way in which they are put together so that the bird passes smoothly from one to another, rising and falling in pitch, varying in volume, until a complete musical composition which is satisfying to the ear has been achieved.

The compass of the song is said to have been measured at almost three octaves, but here again individual singers vary considerably in their ability, and in any case it must be appreciated that there are sopranos and contraltos in the canary world just as in human beings, or perhaps one should say 'tenors' and 'basses' in view of the fact that it is only the males that sing!

The serious beginner in the realm of the Roller canary will find it essential to join a specialist club, where he will learn much more quickly the elements of the song than by reading about it in the pages of a book. At club meetings and song contests he will be able to listen to the birds actually singing, and 'have their tours explained to him by experts as they are being delivered.

BREEDING

The principles of breeding apply no less to the song of the Roller canary than to any other branch of livestock keeping, and if anything, Rollermen are even more insistent on the importance of inbreeding or linebreeding, to preserve the purity of their best singing strains. It has been proved that the inheritance of song is just as definite as that of entirely physical characteristics in type canaries, so that an indifferently bred bird can never be converted into a contest winner no matter how well trained it may subsequently be, whereas a bird of good pedigree, even without training, will sing quite well the pure strains of the type of song it has inherited.

As with type canaries therefore, the quickest route to success is to obtain initial stock from one source, preferably a successful breeder who can be relied upon to supply properly matched pairs or trios, and is willing to give advice regarding their subsequent breeding and training. Birds from such a source, having been linebred, can be relied upon to produce progeny of equal merit to themselves; but on the other hand, breeding from birds purchased at random from various sources, owing to the genetic variability that will be set up, are most likely to produce mainly indifferent songsters, very few of which will possess the virtues of both parental strains.

Young Roller (nestling).

A good deal of skillful selection, followed by backcrossing, inbreeding, and so on, would therefore become necessary before the breeder had established anything like a reliable singing strain of his own.

In this connection it should be noted that it is only from among the cock birds that any positive selection can be made on the basis of song. Hens can only be selected by reference to their pedigrees and from the performances of their nearest male relatives, the process being somewhat analogous, although the sexes are reversed, to the selection of bulls for breeding from a herd of dairy cattle.

The practical aspects of breeding present no special difficulties, for Rollers are amenable to any of the usual systems of management. It must be appreciated however, that when coming into breeding condition perfection of song from the cock birds is no longer to be expected, as they are naturally more excited and tend to over-reach themselves. For this reason many breeders will leave one or two of their best contest birds unmated, and keep them quietly in a separate room away from the hens so that they will be immediately available to act as tutors to the young birds when they are weaned. Close ringing is a universal practice, and all birds intended for contests must be wearing the official rings of one of the recognized specialist societies.

TRAINING

It has already been made abundantly clear that the training of the young cock birds forms an essential aspect of the Roller canary fancy. True it is that well bred youngsters, even without training, will sing quite well, but tuition is just as necessary for them as it is in the case of a good natural athlete, who needs careful training and the guidance of a competent coach to enable him to realize his full potential.

In effect, the training consists of segregating the young cock birds from the remainder of the stock and placing them in a separate room, where they can only hear the song of their tutor. The intention is that, under him, they will learn to sing correctly the various tours, and ultimately reach a stage of proficiency where they are fit to enter for singing contests. The method in which this process is carried out may vary in detail from fancier to fancier, but certain essentials are common to all.

At first it is usual to keep the youngsters in flight cages, at least until after the molt, so that in addition to undergoing the initial stages of learning their song, they are also able to complete their physical development in as natural a manner as possible. Later on they are caged separately, and placed in a special training cabinet where a more careful control can be exercised over them. It is generally advisable to keep the room in which they are undergoing their training darkened down to some extent, in order to enable them to concentrate upon the job in hand and not be distracted in various ways.

During this period a careful 'listening watch' should be kept in order to detect any incipient faults that may be developing in the song, for it is essential to remove at once any bird that utters a harsh, shrill, or any other form of unpleasant note, to avoid it being picked up by the others and thus ruining their own performance. It may well be that in time many will have to be taken away, and only a handful of the very best songsters will remain for the final stages of contest training, but after all, this is no more than happens to the type breeder who only expects a very few of his birds to come near to perfection. The inferior songsters may not necessarily possess very bad faults, but may perhaps be rather limited in the number of tours that they sing, or inclined to repeat certain passages too frequently—errors that would make them unsuitable as contest birds.

The choice of the tutor, or 'schoolmaster' as he is often called, is obviously a matter of paramount importance, and ideally he should be one that is an excellent all round performer with an outstanding delivery of all tours. Naturally such birds are not often available, and the breeder usually has to settle for something less than perfection, but at all events the tutor should be a quiet, steady bird with a deliberate and relaxed performance; the more racy, exuberant type of singer, although perhaps quite exciting to listen to, is rarely suitable for this kind of work.

The old-time mechanical aids for the training of birds are seldom, if ever, employed nowadays, but the modern fancier of course has equipment readily available which was not extant in earlier days. Foremost of these must be reckoned the tape recorder, and there seems no reason at all why tapes of outstanding birds should not be employed for the training of youngsters—the sole reservation being that the quality of reproduction in all but the most expensive instruments is not particularly good.

It must be accepted by the beginner that a full training program, properly carried out, can be quite a complicated undertaking, and is very demanding especially in terms of time.

EXHIBITING

Exhibitions of Roller canaries take the form of singing contests, and for the judge, they are probably the most exacting of their kind in any branch of small livestock keeping. Where visual comparison is the rule any obviously poor quality exhibits can quickly be dismissed, but in the case of the Roller, every bird has to be listened to and the marks that are allocated for the various song tours entered upon an award sheet. This obviously requires both time and close concentration, and the Roller specialist societies see to it that no man is expected to judge any more than a specified number of birds in a day.

Rollers are usually sent out in standard contest cages, which are fitted with wooden shutters to close up the front and keep the bird in darkness when necessary. Well trained birds will commence singing almost as soon as their cages are opened up, and this clearly is a great help to the judge, but a fair chance is given to every bird even though it may mean waiting for some time for it to start singing. The points scored by each bird are totalled up at the end of the contest and the winners are declared.

OFFICIAL STANDARD

It is a peculiarity of this section of the canary fancy that there is no universally recognized standard for the judging of the Roller's song. True it is that such differences as do exist are only ones of emphasis, but it could mean that it is possible for a bird to win under one system of scoring and be lower placed under another. There is, in fact, some evidence to suggest that the adoption of the scoring system which is used in Europe under the C.O.M. would be favored by some fanciers. In general it may be said that some systems tend to favor the 'variety' singer with a large number of tours to its credit, whereas others regard perfection of performance on a more limited repertoire as the criterion.

The Roller canary has a fascination, indeed one might almost say a 'mystique' all of its own and this may be due to the simple fact that comparatively few fanciers are gifted with a sufficiently well-attuned ear to be able to carry out the necessary selection and training with any degree of accuracy. Such obvious attributes as shape and style, color and texture, which are found among the type canaries are fairly readily appreciated by all but the most insensitive person, but minor differences in pitch or tonal quality very easily remain undetected by ears that have become accustomed to the vast cacophany of noise that, unfortunately, is the accepted accompaniment of life today.

INDEX

All page references printed in **bold** refer to photographs.

A

Accessories, Breeding, 52-54
Additional Reading,
  Breeding, 89
  Diseases, 140
Advanced Methods of Breeding, 87
Agate, 262
American Cage Bird Magazine, 260
American Singer Canary, 258-260
  Developing, 258
  Judging, 259
Animal Breeding, 89
Appliances, Other
  Birdroom, 31
  Daily Use, 30-31
Ascheri, M., 269
Aviaries, 17, 18
Awards, Types of, 127

B

Bannerman, D. A., 9
Basic Matings, 51-52
Basic Pigments, 141-143
Basins, Mixing, 54-55
Belgian, **172**, 227, 230-231, 234
Belgishce Bult, 231
Bemrose, E., 96
Bennett, Dr. C. B., 264
Bird Diseases, 140
Birdrooms, 18-25, **19, 20, 23**
  Design, 23-24
  Disinfection, 139-140
  Heating, 25
  Indoor, 20-21
  Lighting, 24

Materials, 24
Outdoor, 21-22
Size, 22-23
Spring Cleaning, 45
Ventilation, 24
Birds of the Atlantic Islands, 9
Blagrove, Josiah, 10, 272
Blakston, W. A., 13, 96, 221
Body Lice, 138-139
Book of Canaries and Cage Birds,
  13, 96
Border Fancy Canaries, **124, 177**
  Chicks, **154, 155**
  Self Blue, **161, 241**
  Self Green, **252**
  Variegated, **251**
  Yellow, **121, 192, 233**
Border Fancy Canary, 150-159
  Breeding, 153-155
  Description, 152
  Exhibiting, 156
  Molting, 156
  Official Standard, 158-159
  Show Cage, **111**, 157
Bossu Belge, 231
Breeding,
  Accessories, 52-54
  Advanced Techniques, 87
  Basic Matings, 51-52
  Condition, 48
  General Precepts, 50-51
  Methods, 86-89
  Practical, 47-72
  Room Register, 54, 55
  System, 49

Theory, 73-89
Time for, 47-48
British Canary, The, 150
Buff, 145, **146**

C

Cage, 25-31
  Construction, 27-28
  Design, **26**, 27
  Finish, 28
  Fittings, 29-30
  Size, 27
Caging, 92-93
Canaries, 14, 65, 150
Canaries, (North America), 247,
    250, 254-255, 257-260
*Canaries, Hybrids and British
    Birds*, 14
Canary,
  Age differences, 147
  Basic Colors, 147
  Early Fanciers, 12-14
  History, 8-16
  Local Breeds, 11-12
  Origin, 8-9
  Recent Mutation, 269-271
  Scientific Status, 9
  Sexing, 148
Canary Book, The, 13
*Canary, Its Varieties, Management
    and Breeding, The*, 13
Canary Matings in Polychrome, 89
Canary Seed, 35
Canthaxanthin, 102, 267
Capsicum annum grossum, 98
Carbohydrates, 33
Care of Young Stock, 71-72
Champion Classes, 119
Cinnamon Inheritance, 82-84
Citron, 269
Clear, 144
Cocks, 48
Color Breeding, 261
Color Classes, List of, 250
Color Feeding, 95-96, 98-99, 102
  History, 96
  Practice, 98-99
  Varieties so Treated, 98
Color and Markings, 141-149

Columbus Fancy, 257-258
Condition Seed, 37
Confederation Ornitologique Mon-
    diale, (C.O.M.) 231, 238, 243,
    246, 280
Corona, **197**
Crest Inheritance, 79-80
Crest Mutation, **217**
Crest x Plainhead, 79
Crested Canary, 214-218
Crested Canary Club, 216
Crystal Palace Show, 179, 183, 195
Cuttlefish, 30

D

"Dead in Shell Chick," 63
Design, Birdroom, 23-24
Dewar Cage Pattern, 157
Dilute, 262
Dimorphic, 268
Diseased Canary, **130**
Diseases, 129, 132-136
  Respiratory, 133-135
  Digestive, 135-136
  Other, 136
Disinfection, 139-140
Dispatch (Exhibiting), 123, 126
Dominant White, 263
Dominant White Ground Color x
    Ground Color, 80-81
Double Pairing, 49
Drawers, Egg Food, 54
Drinkers, 30
Dummy Eggs, 54
Duncker, Dr. Hans, 264
Dutch Frill, **1**, **172**, 239, **242**, 243

E

Early Canary Fanciers, 12-14
Early Canary Variations, 10-11
Egg Box, 54
Eggs, 59
  Binding, 61
  Hatching, 62-64
  Incubation, 61-62
  Laying, 59-61
Environment, 74
Equipment, 25-31
  List of, 31

Exhibiting, 103
  Dispatching to, 123, 126
  Entering for, 118-119, 122
  Preparation for, 122
  Training for, 122
  Types of, 106

F

Fats, 33
Feather Plucking, 72
Feathers, Types of, 91-92
Feeding, 32-40
  Charts, 40-41
  During Molting, 94-95
  Trays, 54
Fife Fancy, 218-219
Fife Fancy Canary Club, 218
  Food, 32-41
  Analysis, 39
  Soft, 38
  Types of, 32-35
Foul, 144
French Canary Birds, 203
Frilled Canaries, 234
  Dutch, 239, 243
  Italian Humpbacked, 243, 246
  Parisian Frill, **172**, 235, 238-239

G

Galloway, Dr. A. R., 214
Gesner, 9, 35
Gibber Italicus, **172**, 243, 246
Gill, A. K., 89, 264
Gloster Fancy Canaries, **58, 60, 62, 63**
  Consort, **112, 228**
  Corona, **228**
  Green Corona, **181**
Gloster Fancy Canary, 195-202
  Breeding, 199-202
  Description, 196-199
  Exhibiting, 201-202
  History, 195
  Molting, 201
  Official Standard, 202
  Show Cage, **111**, 202
Gloster Fancy Canary, The, 175
Gloster Fancy Canary Club, 202
Green Canaries, **245**
Greenstuff, 37

Grit, 38
Grit Containers, 30

H

Hagedoorn, Dr. A. L., 89
Handwashing, **119**
Hatching, 62-64
Heating (Birdroom), 25
Helder, P. J., 262, 270
Hemp Seed, 36
Hens, 49
Heredity, Mechanism of, 74-75
Herniated Air Sacs, **130**
Hervieux, 10, 147, 214, 261, 262, 270
Het Grote Kanarienboek, 89
Historia Animalium, 9
History, Canary, 8-16
  Chart, 15
  Nineteenth Century, 12-14
  Recent, 14-16
Hooded Siskin, 264, 265
Hoppers, Seed, 30
House, C. A., 14, 65, 180, 215
Housing, 17-25

I

Illustrated London News, 12, 13, 221
Improving Points, 88
Inbreeding, 86
Incubation, **60**, 61-62
Indoor Birdroom, 20-21
Initial Stock, 88
Italian Humpbacked Frill, 243, 246

J

Journal of Horticulture, 96
Judging, 127
  Domestic Hartz, 255-257
  Rollers, 254-255

K

Keisel, W., 262
Kerrison, E. H. Jr., 89
Kollen and Brokmeyer, 270

L

Lancashire, 219-220
Lancashire Coppy Canary, **164**
Laying, 59-61
Lee, Miss, 263
Lewer, S. H., 14

Lice, 138
Lighting (Birdroom), 24-25
Linebreeding, 87
Linseed, 37
Lizard Canaries, **206**
    Clear Capped Gold, **244**
Lizard Canary, 203-212
    Breeding, 207-208
    Description, 204-207
    Exhibiting, 209-210
    History, 203
    Molting, 208-209
    Show Cages, 209
    Official Standards, 210-213
Lizard Canary Association (L.C.A.),
    204
Local Societies Members' Shows,
    106
London Fancy, 220-222
London Fancy Club, 221
Lutein, 267
Lutino, 271

M

McLay, J., 195, 196
Management, 41-46
    Daily, 42
    General, 42
    Weekly, 43-44
Matern, Bruno, 264, 268
Maw Seed, 36
Mechanism of Heredity, 74-75
Mendel, Gregor, 76, 222
Mendelian Inheritance in Canaries,
    78-84
Mendelism, 76-77
Mineral Salts, 34
Mixing Basins, 54
Molting, 90-96, 98-99, 102
    Caging During, 92-93
    Conclusion of, 102
    Feeding During, 94-95
    Management During, 93-94
    Process of, 91-92
    Time for, 91-92
Multiple Pairing, 50

N

National American Singers Club,
    260

National Cage Bird Exhibition, 247
Nest and Eggs, **245**
Nesting, 58-59
    Material, 53-54
    Receptacles, **53**
    Troubles, 67-68
New Color Canaries,
    Melanin Dilute Cinnamon, **248**
    Opal Recessive Fawn, **117**
    Recessive White, **185, 256**
New Coloured Canaries, 89, 264
Niger Seed, 36
Norwich Canaries, **180, 189**
    Clear Buff, **109**
    Variegated Yellow, **109**
Norwich Canary, 179, 182-183,
    186-187, 190-191
    Breeding, 187, 190-191
    Description, 183
    Exhibiting, 193
    History, 179, 182-183
    Molting, 191
    Official Standard, 193
    Show Cage, **107**, 193
Norwich Plainhead Canary Club,
    194
Novice Classes, 119
Novice Rule, 119

O

Oats, 37
Oils, 33
Old Varieties Canary Association of
    Great Britain, 220, 226
One Hundred Point Standard,
    254-255
Open Shows, 106
Origin (Canary), 8-9
Origin of Local Breeds, 11-12
Our Canaries, 14, 219, 224
Outbreeding, 87
Outer Birdroom, 21-23

P

Pairing, 49-50, 55-56
Parasites, 137-139
Parisian Frill, **172**, 235, 238-239
Perches, 29-30
Practical Issues, 87-88

Preparation (Exhibition), 122-123
Preventive Measures, 129, 133
Principles of Heredity, 264
Proteins, 33-34

R

Rape Seed, 35-36
Rearing, 64-67
  Difficulties, 67-68
  Food Recipe, 65-67
Recent History (Canary Fancy), 14
Recent Mutations, 269-271
  Ino, 271
  Lipochrome Pastel, 270
  Melanin Pastel, 270
  Satinette, 271
Recessive White, 262
Red Factor Canaries,
  Apricot, **108**
  Bronze Ino Rose Pastel, **105**
  Dimorphic, **168**
  Frosted Bronze Opal, **104, 113, 240**
  Frosted Rose Pastel, **101**
  Lipochrome Pastel, **124**
  Melanin Pastel Apricot, **116**
  Melanin Pastel Red Orange, **165**
  Non-frosted Melanin Pastel, **249**
  Red Orange, **128, 188**
  Rose Ivory, **101**
Red Factor Canary, 263, 268
  Breeding, 266
  Description, 265
  Exhibiting, 267-268
  History, 264
  Molting, 267
Red Mite, 137-138
Ringing, 69-70
Rogerson, Mrs., 195, 196
Roller Canary, 272-280
  Breeding, 276-278
  Description, 274-276
  Exhibiting, 280
  History, 272-274
  Song Standard, 274-275
  Training, 280
Roller Canary (Nestling), **277**
Rubino, 271
Rutgers, A., 89

S

Scale Points,
  Belgian, 231, 234
  Dutch Frill, 243
  Gibber Italicus, 246
  Parisian Frill, 238
Scotch Fancy Canary, 223-224
Second Broods, 70-71
Seed,
  Canary, 35
  Condition, 37
  Hemp, 36
  Linseed, 37
  Maw, 36
  Niger, 36
  Oats, 37
  Rape, 35-36
  Soaked, 65
  Teazle, 36
  Wild, 37
Seed Hoppers, 30
Selection, 85-86
Self, 144
Self Blue, 147
Self Fawn, 147
Serinus canarius canarius, 9
Sexing, 148-149
Show Cage Training, **115**
Show Cages and Cases, **107, 110, 111**
Shows, 106
  Dispatching to, 123, 126
  Entering for, 118-119, 122
  Preparing for, 114-115
  Training for, 114-115
  Types of, 106
Sick Birds, 136-137
Single Pairing, 49
Smith A. W., 195, 196
Smith, Rev. Francis, 13, 221
Soft Food, 38
Song Passages, 274-275
Sooty-black Canary, **232**
Southern Norwich Plainhead Canary Club, 194
Spangle Back, 122
Spangled, 203
Specialist Societies' Show, 106
Spinus cuculatus, 264

Spring Cleaning, 45-46
St. John, Claude, 14, 215, 219, 224
Stewarding, 127
Stroud, Robert, 140
Stroud's Digest on the Diseases of Birds, 140

T

Teazle Seed, 36
Technical Markings, 145
Ticked, 144, 159
Toe Nails (Trimming), **56**
Training (Show), 114-115, 118
Traite de Serins de Canarie, 10
Turn Crown, 214

V

Variation, 84-85
Variegation, 81, 143-144
Varieties from Continental Europe, 227, 230-231, 234-235, 238-239, 243, 246
Varieties of British Origin, Other, 231-224, 226
Ventilation (Birdroom), 24
Vitamins, 34

W

Wallace, R. L., 13

Water, 34-35
  Vessels, 30
Weaning, 68-69
White Canaries, 147
  Dominant, 263
  Inheritance, 80-81
  Recessive, 262-263
Wild Seed, 37

Y

Yellow x Buff, 78
Yorkshire Canaries, **176, 236**
  Blue Variegated, **229, 253**
  Cinnamon Variegated Buff, **100**
  Clear Buff, **225**
  Clear Yellow, **225**
  Self Cinnamon, **184**
  Self Green, **169**
Yorkshire Canary, 160
  Breeding, 166-167, 170
  Description, 162-163, 166
  Exhibiting, 171
  History, 160, 162
  Molting, 170-171
  Official Standards, 174-175
  Show Cage, **110,** 178
Yorkshire Canary Club, 174
Young Canaries, 173
Young Stock, 71-72